T0128291

KNOWING TOMORROW TODAY

GLIMPSES OF THE FUTURE THAT WILL CHANGE YOUR LIFE

MERRICK BROWN

WESTBOW
PRESS®
A DIVISION OF THOMAS NELSON
& ZONDERVAN

This book is a work of non-fiction. Unless otherwise noted, the author and the publisher make no explicit guarantees as to the accuracy of the information contained in this book and in some cases, names of people and places have been altered to protect their privacy.

WestBow Press books may be ordered through booksellers or by contacting:

WestBow Press
A Division of Thomas Nelson & Zondervan
1663 Liberty Drive
Bloomington, IN 47403
www.westbowpress.com
844-714-3454

Headshot by Tashoy Robinson
Book Cover Design by ebooklaunch.com

Scripture quotations marked MSG or "The Message" are taken from The Message. Copyright 1993, 1994, 1995, 1996, 2000, 2001, 2002. Used by permission of NavPress Publishing Group.

Scripture quotations marked NKJV are taken from the New King James Version. Copyright © 1982 by Thomas Nelson, Inc. Used by permission. All rights reserved.

Scripture quotations marked NLT are taken from the Holy Bible, New Living Translation, copyright © 1996, 2004, 2007 by Tyndale House Foundation. Used by permission of Tyndale House Publishers, Inc., Carol Stream, Illinois 60188. All rights reserved.

ISBN: 978-1-6642-9155-3 (sc)
ISBN: 978-1-6642-9157-7 (hc)
ISBN: 978-1-6642-9156-0 (e)

Library of Congress Control Number: 2023902302

Print information available on the last page.

WestBow Press rev. date: 05/31/2023

For my loving wife, Yanouche, and my parents, Rudolph and Angella Brown, who never stopped praying for me.

CONTENTS

FOREWORD

We live in very uncertain times. Fearful times. Unstable times. After what seemed like two years in a science fiction movie, COVID, things are still fearful, uncertain, unstable—maybe even more so!

However, amid all that craziness, there is a God in heaven who loves us, who died for us, and in fact who has not left us alone. Not only that, but He has also given us through His Word "a more sure word of prophecy; whereunto ye do well that ye take heed, as unto a light that shineth in a dark place, until the day dawn, and the day star arise in your hearts" (2 Peter 2:19). And that sure Word, of course, is the Bible.

Hence, Merrick Brown's book about prophecy. Beginning with his own story of an early fascination with Nostradamus, this book tells about his journey to the Bible and the God of the Bible and the hope and promises found in the Bible that point us to our Lord and Savior, Jesus Christ.

In a way, this book is an apologetic, a defense of the faith. But it's also more. It's a personal story about a journey of faith, a journey of hope and trust in God, which in a world where nothing's stable is the greatest hope we can have—the hope found in Jesus.

He writes, "We are helpless to help ourselves. Left to ourselves, we are doomed to suffering, misery, disappointment, pain, death. Like Paul, as we come to grips with our fearful condition, we cry out, 'Oh, what a miserable person I am! Who will free me from this life that is dominated by sin and death?' (Romans 7:24) But there is hope. Because of His boundless love and mercy, God has not abandoned us to utter despair and eternal loss. He has devised and activated a divine plan in which we can find redemption. It is known as the Gospel." And the Gospel is about Jesus.

Amen and amen. From the fall of Lucifer in heaven to the destruction of Lucifer at the end of time and the creation of the new heavens and new earth, Merrick Brown's book covers it all.

Particularly compelling are the last two chapters in which he helps reveal some of the mysteries in the book of Revelation, the last book of the Bible, and the book that, more than any other one in the Bible, tells us how this story will end.

And it ends well, thanks to Jesus, despite the troubling times we live in now.

Clifford R. Goldstein, author and editor, October 2022

ACKNOWLEDGMENTS

I am eternally grateful to my Creator God for calling me out of darkness into His marvelous light, for loving me, and for infusing my life with hope, purpose and meaning.

I owe a debt of gratitude to the editors who worked with me on this project: Clifford R. Goldstein, Lynn Guise, and the editorial team at WestBow Press. Last but certainly not least, I want to thank my wife, Marc-Yriane, for her invaluable critique and constructive advice throughout this project.

"I know who holds tomorrow and I know who holds my hand."
- Ira F. Stanphill

CHAPTER 1

YOU CAN KNOW
THE FUTURE

Buttressed by two great oceans on its east and west and bordered by its good neighbors to its north and south, the American mainland stood fortified, insulated from all forms of turmoil that often took place in the far-flung regions of the world. Or so we thought. This illusory idea was forever ripped from the collective American consciousness on 9/11. On the morning of September 11, 2001, America became a nation transformed when terrorists unleashed a series of deadly attacks at the heart of the nation's financial, political, and military life. At 8:46 a.m., an airliner with ten thousand gallons of fuel plunged into the North Tower of the World Trade Center in New York City. Minutes later, a second passenger jet plowed into the South Tower.[1]

The explosive collisions shook the stately buildings to their core. As if distressed by a mortal wound, the buildings suffered from a huge gaping hole in each, out of which fire and thick smoke—visible from space—billowed. Clearly, the towers were dying. Less than two hours later, the two buildings collapsed into a tangled grave of steel, concrete, ash, and smoldering rubble. Another plane, a third, crashed into the western face of the Pentagon; a fourth, headed perhaps to the United States Capitol, was forced down by American heroes into a field in southern Pennsylvania.[2] *The 9/11 Commission Report* recorded that "more than 2,600 people died at the World Trade Center; 125 died at the Pentagon; 256 died on the four planes. The death toll surpassed that at Pearl Harbor in December 1941."[3]

I was settling in at work in Fort Lauderdale, Florida, when the attacks of September 2001 unfolded. The year before, at the turn of the twentieth century, buoyed by the American dream, I had immigrated to the United States in search of a new life and a new purpose. I remember watching on 9/11, along with billions of viewers around the world, the surrealistic events as they unfolded in real time on television. *How would our lives be changed by the unforeseen tragedy that had been inflicted on America?*

Even prior to our post-9/11 world, the United States national intelligence apparatus had long been regarded as the world's most advanced and capable. No threats or planned attacks on America would have been able to evade the vast far-seeing, all-seeing electronic eyes and ears of the National Security Agency (NSA)—or so we thought. Indeed, it turns out that US government intelligence agencies had received ominous warnings of a potential attack on the US homeland. According to the 9/11 Commission, "During the Spring and Summer of 2001, US intelligence agencies received a stream of warnings that al Qaeda planned, as a report put it, 'Something very, very, very big.' Director of Central Intelligence George Tenet told us, 'The system was blinking red.'"[4]

Could it be though as some believe, that the warning about the 9/11 attacks had gone out decades, even centuries, before they took place? Had someone foreseen that tragic day in American history and tried to warn us? In fact, in the days and weeks following the attacks, the top word that trended on Google was, believe it or not, *Nostradamus.*

NOSTRADAMUS?

In a September 18, 2001, *New York Times* article titled "Suddenly, It's Nostradamus, the Best Seller," Emily Eakin writes that during the week of the 9/11 attacks, among the twenty-five best-selling books on Amazon were three editions of Nostradamus's prophecies.[5] Eakin's article states that following the attacks, in a desperate need to find information and an explanation for the 9/11 attacks, "interest in the doomsday prophecies of Nostradamus was unprecedented ... from people who aren't familiar with Nostradamus and suddenly want to read him."[6] Amid the online chatter, which circulated within hours after the tragic attack, many became convinced that a sixteenth-century medical doctor and soothsayer named Nostradamus had somehow relayed crucial intelligence about the attacks in these lines, which they claimed were taken from one of his quatrains in 1654:

> In the city of God there will be a great thunder,
> Two brothers torn apart by Chaos,
> While the fortress endures ...

Enthusiasts who decrypted this obscure poem say that if we take "the city of God" to be a reference to modern-day New York City, then "the two brothers torn apart by Chaos" are the Twin Towers that were reduced to piles of steel, glass, ash, and smoke by "a great thunder" or explosion. Nostradamian interpreters also creatively inferred from the poem that the phrase "the fortress endures" points to the Pentagon, the fortress-like headquarters of the US Defense Department, which though damaged on its western side remained structurally intact. Devotees of the French psychic also pointed to these verses (century 6, quatrain 97) as another Nostradamus prophecy about 9/11:

Two steel birds will fall from the sky on the Metropolis.
The sky will burn at forty-five degrees latitude.
Fire approaches the great city.

Nostradamians maintain that the "two steel birds" that "fall from the sky on the Metropolis" are the two steel towers that, after succumbing to the explosive force of thousands of gallons of ignited jet fuel, buckled and fell from their crowning heights amid the princely skyscrapers of the New York City skyline. Perhaps what is most alluring about this purported prophecy is that geographically the New York City metropolitan area does lie between latitude forty and forty-five degrees. The poem suggests that the Metropolis burns at forty-five degrees latitude.

Could it be then that Michel Nostradamus foresaw the 9/11 attacks centuries earlier, or are these poems simply gibberish concocted by internet conspiracy theorists?

CONFESSIONS OF A NOSTRADAMIAN

There was a time in my life beginning in the 1980s when I was a devoted follower of Nostradamus and his prophecies. Through the tumultuous days of the sixth grade in Jamaica—in a world without color television, the internet, on-demand TV, streaming services, or social media—my friends and I would regularly convene during lunchtime for our daily movie forums to critique the latest kung fu, horror, and action flicks that we had seen on local television. My love affair with the French psychic was sparked in one of these forums when, one day, a classmate enthusiastically reported that a documentary film, *The Man Who Saw Tomorrow*, was to be aired on local TV at midnight. The film, he said, was about a mysterious man named Nostradamus who supposedly could see into the future and had made some startling predictions of biblical proportions about World War III, Armageddon, and the end of the world. I went off into a frenzy of excitement that skyrocketed to fever pitch levels because, even in those early years, I was already intensely attuned to future things.

For as long as I can remember, our black-and-white television set became an altar of worshipful fascination for me. The dawning and the closing of each day required that I would kneel on our living room carpet in contemplative silence for an hour at least, enraptured in the enchanting glory of TV bliss. During this daily ritual, I was able to absorb all the sights, sounds, and flickering images of history that came into our living room from around the world. Back in those days, I was keenly aware that a Cold War chill had descended over Europe decades before, its iron curtain symbolically dividing the world into East and West, freezing relations between the Soviet Union and the United States.

I understood from very early the significance of Jamaica's proximity to Fidel Castro's Cuba, only ninety miles away. I knew that this standoff between the villainous red communists and our friendly, good neighbor to the north, the United States, was at best tenuous. The possibility that an international incident could have been triggered at any moment was very real as each superpower had thousands of intercontinental ballistic nuclear missiles in their arsenals and aimed squarely at each other. The result of all this was that I became fascinated by doomsayers and their endgame scenarios of where they thought the international political chess game was headed. So in addition to my growing up amid Cold War tensions, my worldview was also molded by a potpourri of Bible prophecy hearsay mixed in with the occasional dashes of apocalyptic end-of-the-world movies. The great battle of Armageddon was, I thought, soon to be fought by the world's superpowers; thus, I was anxious to hear what Michel Nostradamus had to say about it all.

I'm not alone in a curiosity about the future. The futurist Stephan A. Schwartz stated that "there is no siren whose call is quite so exquisite as the music of the future. For as long as writing has existed, there are records showing we have sought to know its form."[7]

Embedded in the human psyche is a powerful incurable thirst to know tomorrow. We have all wondered about what fortunes and future outcomes await us. We sense that the choices we make daily, for good and for ill, individually and collectively, are all coalescing and adding to the tapestry of a story that will manifest as our destiny.

Today, in an attempt to read the tea leaves of their lives, many people consult horoscopes, tarot cards, or even fortune cookies. Others pay mediums, psychics, or fortune tellers. Some years ago, I read a fanciful story about an internet bot called Web Bot—a computer algorithm originally created to predict stock market trends that supposedly had the ability to predict the future. As it scanned and analyzed millions of news articles, social media platforms, forums, blogs, and other forms of internet chatter, it was suggested that perhaps this internet bot could use this data to predict future events. However, most critics agree that a computer algorithm infused with artificial intelligence or machine-learning capabilities would be no more capable of predicting a natural disaster than would a Google search.[8]

One thing though that this internet bot confirmed is that people are fearful and apprehensive about the future. Plagued by the many uncertainties of our complex technological age, most people would love to have an inkling of what lies ahead, to have even a glimpse of tomorrow today. Schwartz accurately infers that "in times of stress, when your relationship is changing, or your job is disappearing, or you are faced with a fateful choice, it would be extraordinarily helpful to get even a glimpse of what lies before."[9]

We live in an age of great technological progress with daunting existential challenges, daily spinning beyond our capacity to solve. Writing in *Fortune* magazine, Quentin Hardy lamented, "What is going on here? We were, by almost any measure of space and time, a group others would kill to become ... we are longer lived and with access to more knowledge and experiences than any other king or pope who has come before ... this much luck should make us hug ourselves with delight ... the daily advances in science and technology lend hope that on balance things are getting better. Except that we do not feel that way."[10] But of course, we are not hugging ourselves with delight. A specter of uncertainty hovers over our collective futures. The moral fabric of society seems to be disintegrating before our eyes, and many people openly wonder what kind of world our children and grandchildren will inherit with the downward spiral each generation seems to be taking.

Ultimately, a desire to know the future speaks to a deeper, more powerful yearning that we all have for meaning, certainty, and continuity. We want to know that, somehow, our lives matter and that we will not be forgotten in the maelstrom and clutter of the human continuum. As he pondered his mortality, renowned Russian author Leo Tolstoy wrote in his book *A Confession*, "My question, the question that had brought me to the edge of suicide when I was fifty years old, was the simplest of question lying in the soul of every human being ... the question was this: What will come of what I do today and tomorrow? What will come of my entire life ... is there any meaning in my life that will not be destroyed by my inevitably approaching death?"[11] As we live, we subconsciously are seeking for an affirmation, an assurance that our brief time here and the contributions we make will live on if only in the memories and the storied record of those whom we leave behind.

As we gaze deeper into the night sky sprinkled with its billions of gleaming galaxies and shimmering far-off stars, we are more than awed by the enormity and grandeur of the universe that hovers above us like a shining gallery with an intricately designed master work. We are at times almost overwhelmed by the thought that our existence on a minuscule planet in the corner of an average spiraling galaxy seems almost negligible in comparison to the unending vast expanse of space. We feel almost powerless as we sense that we are caught up in something that is infinitely beyond our capacity to control and maybe even to understand, ever!

We observe that stars like our sun are born, shine for a time in all their radiant glory, and then as if taking their last gasp for breath, suddenly expand only to be dwarfed later by death. Like stars that are born and then die, we too have come to realize the transient nature of our own lives. We realize that someday we too will make the transition to death. Yet we hold out hope that perhaps one day, in some shape or form, we could truly be immortal. And so instinctively, we crave a sort of flash-forward to the future because we sense that these glimpses of tomorrow might just provide us with rational, cogent explanations for our purpose and destiny.

It was this inherent desire for a glimpse of tomorrow that fueled and nurtured my misplaced obsession with Nostradamus that lasted for many years. His name alone, *Nostradamus,* suggested an eerie otherworldliness. It had a seductive, bewitching quality that somehow gave credence to his purported prophetic ability. True believers in the sixteenth-century psychic's prognostic ability contend that he accurately predicted wars, natural disasters, and the rise and fall of many of history's great dictators and their empires. They believe that in his most famous extensive collections of predictions called *Les Prophéties,* he foresaw the atomic age, the space age, and the digital age. They further contend that buried deep within his voluminous prophetic writings is a warning of a stupendous global crisis just before us.

THE 1999 PROPHECY

By July 1999, after a spectacularly failed Nostradamus prediction, I had lost all faith in his ability to predict the future. That year, while many of my youthful contemporaries gyrated in a heady yearlong millennial dance, partying away because it was 1999, I was frequently racked with bouts of self-doubt as I reflected on the twists and turns that my short life had then taken. At twenty-two, I still had not figured out what I wanted to do with my life. For me, the road ahead seemed hazy and murky. A cloud of uncertainty hovered over my future. The truth was that I was scared, and I was not alone.

Time magazine's January 18, 1999, cover captured the general mood and anxiety that pervaded the times. "The End of the World!?!: Y2K Insanity! Apocalypse Now! Will Computers Melt Down? Will Society? A Guide to Millennium Madness." For those not old enough to remember the strange days of 1999, the so-called Y2K computer bug was not merely something conjured up out of thin air by crooked millennium prophets and alarmists. The computer programming glitch was potentially seen as a real-world problem by governments, computer experts, private companies, and ordinary citizens.

As all sectors of society raced to become Y2K compliant, there was much trepidation that a Y2K digital apocalypse could possibly trigger the breakdown of everything. Amid the rampant forebodings of the approaching third millennium, a palpable excitement among Nostradamians arose as many of us wondered how this quatrain (century 10, quatrain 72), Nostradamus's most famous prediction of the twentieth century, would come to pass:

> The year 1999, the seventh month,
> From the sky shall descend a great King of Terror,
> To revive the great king of the Angolmois,
> Before and after, Mars shall reign for a good cause.

For decades, the famous so-called 1999 prophecy had garnered much attention because it was a rarity for the psychic to use a literal year in any of his predictions. At the time, many believed that the quatrain predicted the rise of Nostradamus's third antichrist, the so-called great King of Terror, in July 1999. Some interpreters excitedly and somewhat deluded pointed out that if the letters of the phrase *Angolmois* were rearranged, it would almost pass as an anagram for *Mongolois*. As a result, there was speculation that perhaps Nostradamus's third antichrist would arise from Asia or the Middle East following a global Y2K catastrophe.

Of course, we now know that the antichrist did not make his

appearance in 1999 as had been expected, nor was there a global Y2K societal collapse on January 1, 2000. The 1999 prophecy had captivated my young imagination for years, and when it failed to come to pass, I lost all faith in Nostradamus's ability to predict the future. In hindsight, I had been very fortunate. I had been freed from a deception that had held me captive for many years. Yet despite the spectacular failure of predictions like the 1999 prophecy, many people are still charmed today into believing that Nostradamus saw the future.

John Hogue, a popular American Nostradamian in the late twentieth century, stated with great naivety that the quatrains of Nostradamus are "still defying explanation," despite evidence to the contrary that several quatrains have failed to meet their expected fulfillment. James Randi, the so-called debunker of New Age quackery, explained that Nostradamus remains popular today because he "has been embraced by non-history. Any number of newspapers and magazine accounts, television documentaries, reference books, and textbooks assert the legitimacy of his prophetic powers as if they had never come under serious questioning."[19]

PSYCHIC HOGWASH

For centuries, historians have painstakingly examined Nostradamus's extensive collection of "prophecies" and have found them wanting. In his book *Nostradamus and His Prophecies,* regarded by historians as the most comprehensive, definitive scholarly investigation on the life of Nostradamus, Edgar Leoni concluded that "at best it can be said of Nostradamus as a prophet is that he occasionally had a successful 'vision' of what would happen, but never of *when* anything would happen."[20]

Still, we have to ask what Leoni meant when he said that the psychic "occasionally had a successful 'vision' of what would happen." How do we explain the many seemingly "successful" Nostradamus "prophetic hits" that have so often captivated some of history's most brilliant minds?

The answer lies in an ingenious system of divination that Nostradamus had used to construct his prophecies. These ancient divination techniques predate Nostradamus and are still used by many modern psychics today, and to great effect. Leoni writes that Nostradamus's "visions," especially those written in quatrain form, are intentionally obscure, enigmatic, and ambiguous and as a result "lend themselves to repeated interpretations, so they never seem to be out of date."[21]

Another divination technique that Nostradamus employed to phenomenal success is his profusion of predictions about the future. The psychic wrote, "I have composed books of prophecies, of which each contains one hundred astronomical quatrains of prophecies … they are perpetual prophecies, for they extend from now to the year 3797."[22]

Leoni also notes that the bulk of the psychic's prophecies "owe much of their incredible reputation to their rather catastrophic content."[23] In other words, many of Nostradamus's predictions deal with disasters of some sort, usually "plagues, earthquakes, wars, floods, invasions, murders, droughts, battles, and many other themes."[24]

All of this would lead us to conclude that Nostradamus's much-heralded predictions are hoaxes, coincidences, or "mistranslations, misinterpretations, and creative extrapolations" of his writings. Let's go back to the poem I shared at the beginning of this chapter.

> In the city of God there will be a great thunder,
> Two brothers torn apart by Chaos,
> While the fortress endures … ("Nostradamus 1654")

Many believed that this quatrain was a prophecy by Nostradamus about the 9/11 terrorist attacks. The problem with this prediction is that it is a hoax. Notice that the poem is dated "Nostradamus 1654."

However, Nostradamus died in the year 1566. The quatrain was, in fact, lifted from an essay written in 1996 entitled "Nostradamus: A Critical Analysis," by Neil Marshall, who was a college student. After Marshall posted his essay online, elements of it took on a life of their own. Marshall "admits to inventing the quatrain to illustrate, quite ironically in light of the way it was subsequently misused—how a Nostradamus-like verse can be so cryptically couched as to lend itself to whatever interpretation one wishes to make."[25]

But how do we explain this quatrain (century 6, quatrain 97) that supposedly was another 9/11 prediction attributed to Nostradamus?

> Two steel birds will fall from the sky on the Metropolis.
> The sky will burn at forty-five degrees latitude.
> Fire approaches the great city ...

Actually, the complete online version of this quatrain reads,

> Two steel birds will fall from the sky on the Metropolis.
> The sky will burn at forty-five degrees latitude.
> Fire approaches the great city
> Immediately a huge, scattered flame leaps up.
> Within months, rivers will flow with
> Blood. The undead will roam the earth for a little time.

It was extrapolated from this quatrain that the "two steel birds" that "fall from the sky on the Metropolis" were the World Trade Center's Twin Towers on 9/11. Here the quatrain also seems to pinpoint the location of the disaster. It mentions that "the sky will burn at forty-five degrees latitude." However, take a look at century 6, quatrain 97, as it is transcribed from Nostradamus's original writings.

At forty-five degrees the sky will burn,
Fire to approach the great new city:
In an instant a great scattered flame will leap up,
When one will want to demand proof of the
Normans.

Significant differences exist between the online version and Nostradamus's original quatrain, in which Nostradamus makes no mention of "two steel birds falling from the sky." Nor did he predict that "the undead will roam the earth for a little time." Clearly, the online version of the quatrain underwent several imaginative and creative revisions for dramatic effect.

PSYCHICS AND BIBLICAL PROPHETS

The truth is there is nothing of prophetic value in Nostradamus's writings. Perhaps what is most disconcerting is that many Nostradamians are quite unaware that Nostradamus himself acknowledged as much about his predictions. Writing to King Henry of France about his quatrains, Nostradamus confessed, "Indeed, someone, who would do well to blow his nose, may reply that the rhythm is easy as the sense is difficult. That, O Most Humane king, is because most of the prophetic quatrains are so ticklish that there is no making way through them, nor is there any interpreting of them."[26]

As he stared nightly into his brass bowl filled with water and recited his occult incantations, Nostradamus may have seen something. Whatever he saw, he did not see the future. It is quite telling that for many years, this clever stinging review of *Les Prophéties* was circulated throughout France by some of Nostradamus's scholarly contemporaries: "Nostra damus cum falsa damus, nam fallere nostrum est; et cum falsa damus, nil nisi nostra damus." Translated from Latin into English, it reads: "We give that which is our own when we give false things: for it is our nature to deceive; and when we give false things, we give our own things."[27]

Jean Dixon, a famous twentieth-century psychic, declared that "the same spirit that worked through Isaiah and John the Baptist works through me."[28] She also "defended Nostradamus's gift saying that she was convinced that he was a man of God."[29] In the Bible, the word *prophet* is most often translated from the Hebrew word *roeh*, from a root word that means "to see." There are also instances when the word *prophet* is translated from the Hebrew word *nabi*, which means "to speak forth." In this sense, the biblical prophets not only foretold the future but also proclaimed God's special messages. Historian LeRoy Froom writes that, unlike psychics like Nostradamus and Jean Dixon, the biblical prophet "is a channel of communication and not the source thereof. He is a speaker, or spokesman, for God. His message is not his own but comes from a higher source. He is a seer, seeing things outside of the domain of natural sight."[30]

As it turns out, the Bible has very stringent qualifications for its prophets. Prophets after the biblical mold were required to get their predictions right. Outside of conditional prophecy, which depended on the actions of the people, if a prophet said that an event was going to happen, it would happen. This requirement alone disqualifies Jean Dixon and Nostradamus as prophets cut in the biblical mold.

Nostradamus would also be excluded from this select group of men and women because of his practice of astrology and the occult. There is an abundance of evidence in his quatrains that suggests that the psychic was highly influenced by a fourth-century occult book called *De Mysteriis Aegyptiorum*, a collection of magic incantations and spells written by a fourth-century philosopher and mystic named Iamblichus. The Bible strongly condemns astrology and the occult. In Deuteronomy, the prophet Moses gave this strict warning to the people that they should stay away from these practices: "Do not let your people practice fortune-telling, or use sorcery, or interpret omens [astrology], or engage in witchcraft, or cast spells, or function as mediums or psychics, or call forth the spirits of the dead. Anyone who does these things is detestable to the Lord" (Deuteronomy 18:10–12 NLT).

So this question remains: is there any way for us to tap into the future, to catch glimpses of tomorrow today? In H. G. Well's 1895 science fiction novella *The Time Machine*, the story's protagonist creates a time machine that enables him to travel, purposely and selectively, millions of years into the future. Wells's time traveler has a front-row seat to the earth and humanity's unfolding "progress." If we are to believe that science fiction will one day become science fact, perhaps in the not too distant future, humanity will be able to travel in a machine through the wormholes of space and time to arrive at futures that we have long sought but were always out of our grasp. But perhaps the key to unlocking the future will not involve traversing space and time in a machine but in a rediscovery and reexamination of ancient records of the past.

The truth is that in our hectic, modern, technological world, there is much ancient knowledge that has been lost. After I was freed from my cultic Nostradamian fixation, for many years I still continued my personal quest to find the door that would lead me to tomorrow. What I eventually found was so powerful and earth-shattering that it upended my worldview and caused me to see the world in a new light.

Throughout the centuries, the Bible has come to mean different things to different people. There is perhaps no other book in history that has been more influential. As the best-selling book of all time, the Bible is a record of God's acts in human history. Sir Isaac Newton, the man who invented calculus and formulated the theory of universal gravity, stated that "there are more sure marks of authenticity in the Bible than in any profane history."[32] This was a profound statement, especially when we think of all the ancient historical masterpieces that have come down to us. Composed of sixty-six books and written by forty-four different men over a period of 1,500 years, the Bible is remarkable because of its cohesive unity and consistency. It can be trusted as an authoritative, authentic, and reliable record of God's dealings with humanity.

I have discovered, as have millions of others, that the prophecies of the Bible provide a clear and concrete roadmap of the future. Biblical expert Norman Geisler reaffirms that "the Bible is the only book in the world that has precise, specific predictions that were made hundreds of years in advance and that were literally fulfilled ... the problem with Nostradamus and so many other so-called psychics is that their predictions are often very enigmatic, ambiguous, and inaccurate."[31] Hence, the prophecies of hope outlined in the successive chapters of this book literally have the potential to change your life—forever.

Does this all sound like something fantastical, far-fetched, unreal, too good to be true—maybe even bordering on the ridiculous? As someone with a mind that is rooted in rationality and common sense, I know exactly how you feel. It is my hope though that you will allow your curiosity to get the better of you and that you will take some time to explore realities that have brought hope to so many. The good news is that whatever you thought that tomorrow's world would be, the future might vastly exceed your brightest hopes, your wildest dreams, and your greatest expectations.

CHAPTER 2

THE NEXT SUPERPOWER

The exiles—men, women, and children—wept uncontrollably as they realized that they would never see their homeland again. Just days before, Jerusalem had surrendered to the Babylonians. With the news of the devastating defeat of his most trusted ally, Egypt, King Jehoiakim of Judah capitulated to the demands of the Babylonian king, Nebuchadnezzar, after he laid siege to Jerusalem. After the fall of the city, the Babylonians looted the Jewish temple of all its sacred treasures and deported members of the Jewish royal family and nobility to Babylon. Among the Jewish nobility who made the journey across the Fertile Crescent of the Arabian Desert to Babylon were Daniel and his teenaged friends, Shadrach, Meshach, and Abednego.

Known to the Jews as the hammer of the whole earth (Jeremiah 50:23), the Babylonian menace, which had long terrorized the nations of the Mediterranean, had finally made its way to Jerusalem's door. Several years before, by allying themselves with the Medes, mountain people from northern Iran, the Babylonians had thrown off the political yoke of the Assyrian Empire. After successfully destroying the ancient Assyrian metropolitan centers of Nineveh and Nimrud, Babylon became the undisputed superpower in the region.[1]

As Daniel and his friends traveled to Babylon, they may have recalled that several Jewish prophets had foretold the doom of

Jerusalem. Remarkably, some eighty years before, the prophet Isaiah had related to King Hezekiah, the ruler at this time, that "the time is coming when everything in your palace—all the treasurers stored up by your ancestors ... will be carried off to Babylon. Nothing will be left ... some of your own sons will be taken away into exile. They will become eunuchs who will serve in the palace of Babylon's king" (Isaiah 39:5–7 NLT). Daniel certainly would have known that Isaiah's prophecy was being fulfilled.

Again, one can imagine that before drifting off to sleep at night, Daniel could hear the vengeful, muffled whispers of several Jewish men who plotted a futile insurrection. Or as he listened to the sobbing prayers of the women, with tears in his eyes, Daniel surely thought of his own mother, remembering that she had often prayed, "Must my son be a captive in the court of a heathen king? Then let me so train him that he will be true to the God of his fathers." Now as he looked up at the desert night sky, Daniel probably found himself praying to the God of his fathers and resolved that he would remain true to this God even though separated from his family and country.

DANIEL THE PROPHET

The story of Daniel, a Jewish exile who served as a statesman and administrator in ancient Babylon during the reigns of Nebuchadnezzar II and Cyrus of Medo-Persia, is recorded in the Bible. Born into a prominent Jewish family circa 623 BC, Daniel was a Jewish prince among exiles who, during a siege of the city, were taken from Jerusalem to Babylon by King Nebuchadnezzar 605 BC. Many are well acquainted with the exciting accounts of Daniel's deliverance from the lion's den and of the miraculous rescue of his three friends, Shadrach, Meshach, and Abednego, from King Nebuchadnezzar's fiery furnace.

As a statesman in ancient Babylon, Daniel was esteemed for

his integrity, wisdom, judgment, and intelligence. But as a prophet, he predicted with remarkable precision the rise and fall of several world empires in history. Flavius Josephus, a court historian to three successive Roman emperors, remarked that the prophet Daniel was "one of the greatest of the prophets ... for he did not only prophesy of future events, as did the other prophets, but he also determined the time of their accomplishment."[2]

Several of history's most illustrious luminaries were often transfixed by Daniel's book of prophecy. Most notably, English mathematician and physicist Sir Isaac Newton predicted that "about the time of the end, a body of men will be raised up who will turn their attention to the prophecies and insist upon their literal interpretation." Indeed, what is most startling about the book of Daniel is that its author outlines with stunning accuracy the history of the world from ancient Babylon to the "time of the end," something that Nostradamus didn't come close to doing.

Daniel's prophecies are unique in that while many of the biblical prophets addressed the contemporary issues and occasionally gave "flash pictures" of the future, the book of Daniel provides a comprehensive prophetic outline of history that culminates with the setting up of a future, global kingdom that will last forever. Even though it was written some twenty-five centuries ago by a Jewish exile living in ancient Babylon, the book of Daniel continues to captivate millions around the world because, more than anything else, it provides us with a glimpse of the destiny of humanity, inspiring millions with hope.

THE UNIVERSITY OF BABYLON

The story of Daniel and his friends, Shadrach, Meshach, and Abednego, begins with their arrival in Babylon after their four-hundred-mile trek from Jerusalem. The exiles would certainly have been shell-shocked by the city's imposing architecture and alien culture. Renowned for its enormous wealth and power, Babylon was a wonder of the ancient world. The Greek historian Herodotus, who visited the city in the fifth century BC, wrote that Babylon was the strongest and most notable city of the ancient world and that it was "designed like no other city known to us."[3]

During his forty-three-year reign, Nebuchadnezzar undertook a massive building program in which he constructed an array of temples, palaces, fortresses, ziggurats, and immense gold statues—the scope and size of which rivaled the building projects of the Egyptian pharaohs. It is also believed that the legendary Hanging Gardens of Babylon, one of the Seven Great Wonders of the ancient world, was also located inside the city.

Surrounded by a moat that was wide and deep, the city was considered almost impenetrable by enemy forces. The ancient metropolis was secured by massive iron and brass gates and had an outer and inner double wall defense system. Herodotus records that the outer walls of the city were so wide that it had space for two, four-horse chariots to ride alongside each other.[4] In the event that the city ever came under siege, the inhabitants of Babylon were said to have had enough food supplies to last them for twenty years.

Upon arrival, Daniel and his friends were enrolled in the university of Babylon. It was the policy of the Babylonians to select the smartest, best-looking, and most gifted young men from the royal and leading families of their conquered nations to train them in all the culture, language, literature, and sciences of Babylon. After a three-year training period, the foreigners were usually installed as administrators in Babylon or in their native lands.

As many students know, one of the adjustments of college life is cafeteria food, and for Daniel and his friends in ancient Babylon, this was no different. Daniel records that King Nebuchadnezzar assigned the university students "a daily ration of the best food and wine from his own kitchens" (Daniel 1:5 NLT). Talk about receiving the royal treatment on campus! We are told though that Daniel decided that he would not "defile himself by eating the food and wine given to them by the king" (Daniel 1:8 NLT). He reached out to the king's chief of staff in order to get his permission to eat other things instead.

Why would anyone complain about cafeteria food if the menu afforded the opportunity to eat like a king? Why would eating from the royal Babylonian menu "defile" the young men? For Daniel, there was a theological reason that had practical health implications. Daniel refused to eat food prepared in the pagan king's kitchens because of his fidelity to the God of his fathers. In the history of Daniel's people, as the children of Israel came out of Egypt, their God instructed them through Moses (Exodus 15) that if they obeyed His voice, they would not suffer from the common diseases that plagued Egyptian society. Indeed, scientists today have confirmed after examining Egyptian mummies that the ancient Egyptians were afflicted with several of our modern diseases that were largely brought on by their diet.

According to Near Eastern scholar William H. Shea, Babylonian cuneiform records reveal that the Babylonian diet included a steady supply of pork and several exotic delicacies.[5] It may come as a surprise to some, but Jewish dietary laws included pigs in the same category as camels, bats, moles, rats, lizards, and snakes—critters deemed unclean or unfit for human consumption (Leviticus 11). These unclean foods have the tendency to defile, pollute, or sicken us. Bats often carry rabies, lizards carry salmonella, and pigs host several harmful microscopic critters. Shea also notes that Daniel may have wanted to stay away from the Babylonians' cafeteria food because it may have been offered to idols, and it was probably not kosher.[6]

Determined that he would not sicken himself with the Babylonian cafeteria food, Daniel was able to convince Nebuchadnezzar's chief of staff, who had responsibility for the young men's care and development, to test them for ten days on water and a plant-based diet to see if they would remain as healthy as the other students. Remarkably, at the end of the ten days, "Daniel and his three friends looked healthier and better nourished than the young men who had been eating the food assigned by the king. So after that, the attendant fed them only vegetables instead of the food and wine provided for the others" (Daniel 1:14–16 NLT).

The Hebrew boys also excelled during their three years of university training. They had an "unusual aptitude for understanding every aspect of literature and wisdom. And God gave Daniel the special ability to interpret the meanings of visions and dreams" (Daniel 1:17 NLT). At their final examination, King Nebuchadnezzar conducted the interviews himself, and he was very impressed by the young men's wisdom, intelligence, and judgment. He soon realized that the graduates were much smarter than all of the advisors in his kingdom, so according to Daniel 1:20, he appointed Daniel, Shadrach, Meshach, and Abednego to serve on his advisory council.

A DREAM OF WORLD EMPIRES

Daniel records that one night, about the year 603 BC, King Nebuchadnezzar "had such disturbing dreams that he couldn't sleep" (Daniel 2:1). Calling for his chief advisors, his magicians, enchanters, sorcerers, and astrologers, the king told them that he "had such dreams that he couldn't sleep" (Daniel 2:1 NLT). Even though some people "continue to mine them for clues to their inner lives, creative insight, and even hints of the future,"[7] most of us usually don't think twice about the occasional nightmare. However, for the Babylonians and other ancient peoples, dreams were believed to be omens or prophecies from the gods. Babylonian society, in particular, welcomed dreams as messages from their gods, and the people would sometimes go far as to spend all night in a temple to receive divine messages.[8]

Startled by King Nebuchadnezzar's usual request, his advisors asked that he first tell them the dream so that they could give him an interpretation (Daniel 2:4). Like many fortune tellers and astrologers today, these ancient Babylonian wise men were frauds. William Shea states that "each of these classes of wise men needed something to work with. The astrologers used the stars; the diviners used sheep livers; others used different signs in nature that signaled something to them—such as the birth of an animal with a congenital deformity."[9] King Nebuchadnezzar was adamant. "I am serious about this," he warned. "If you don't tell me what my dream was and what it means, you will be torn limb from limb, and your houses will be demolished into heaps of rubble! But if you tell me what I dreamed and what the dream means, I will give you many wonderful gifts and honors. Just tell me the dream and what it means!" (Daniel 2:5–6 NLT). Mesopotamian kings were not known for making idle threats. The Babylonians and the Assyrians were well known in antiquity for cutting up the bodies of their enemies and burning their houses.[10] So the Babylonian wise men were in a serious quandary: produce or die!

As they entreated the king to spare their lives, Nebuchadnezzar's advisors told him that what he was requesting was beyond the scope of their job description. With frantic pleadings, they asserted that only the gods were able to relate to the king his dream (Daniel 2:11). These charlatans were right. What the king was asking of them was humanly impossible. Enraged, the king made a decree that all the wise men in Babylon were to be exterminated.

As members of Nebuchadnezzar's advisory council, Daniel and his friends, Shadrach, Meshach, and Abednego, were also marked for death. When Arioch, the commander of the king's royal guard, came looking for them, Daniel tactfully asked him the reason for the hasty and harsh decree. After Arioch had explained, Daniel bravely sought an audience with King Nebuchadnezzar and requested that he give him time to discern the dream and provide an interpretation.

This was a courageous move on Daniel's part because there were no guarantees that he would have been able to unravel the mystery of the king's request. But perhaps Daniel took courage from the story of his ancestor Joseph in Egypt who, with the help of the God of his fathers, had been able to provide an Egyptian pharaoh with divine insight about his troubling night visions. Daniel may have been encouraged by Joseph's words that "interpreting dreams is God's business" (Genesis 40:8 NLT).

And so, Daniel informed his friends that what they most urgently needed to do was "to ask the God of heaven to show them His mercy by telling them the secret, so they would not be executed along with the other wise men of Babylon" (Daniel 2:18 NLT). After they had petitioned their God in prayer, Daniel records that the mystery concerning Nebuchadnezzar's dream was revealed to him that night by his God in a dream (Daniel 2:19).

Later, as Daniel stood before the king to reveal the meaning of his dream, Nebuchadnezzar asked with amazement, "Is it true? Can you tell me what my dream was and what it means?" (Daniel 2:26, NLT). Daniel confessed to Nebuchadnezzar that there is not a mortal alive who could uncover the mystery of the king's dream but assured him that "there is a God in heaven who reveals secrets, and he has shown King Nebuchadnezzar what will happen in the future" (Daniel 2:27 NLT).

Nebuchadnezzar must have been intrigued by the confidence that this Hebrew exile had in his God, yet it may have bothered him that one of his own native Babylonian dream specialists had not stepped forward to provide him with the answers he sought.

Historian LeRoy Froom writes,

> Nebuchadnezzar knew the god Nabu as the patron of wisdom, the revealer of secrets, and the messenger of the gods, recorder of the destinies of mankind on the Tablets of Fate; yet Marduk himself, the keeper of the Tablets, presided over the council of the gods every New Year, when the fates were determined. Why, then, could not the wise men of Babylon, the servants of Marduk, or of his son Nabu, tell the king

what this captive Hebrew youth could reveal? Was
Marduk not as powerful as Daniel's God?[11]

As he related to King Nebuchadnezzar what he had dreamed,
Daniel tells the king,

> While Your Majesty was sleeping, you dreamed
> about coming events in your vision, Your Majesty,
> you saw standing before you a huge, shining statue
> of a man. It was a frightening sight. The head of the
> statue was made of fine gold. Its chest and arms were
> silver, its belly and thighs were bronze, its legs were
> iron, and its feet were a combination of iron and
> baked clay. As you watched, a rock was cut from a
> mountain, but not by human hands. It struck the feet
> of iron and clay, smashing them to bits. The whole
> statue was crushed into small pieces of iron, clay,
> bronze, silver, and gold. Then the wind blew them
> away without a trace, like chaff on a threshing floor.
> But the rock that knocked the statue down became
> a great mountain that covered the whole earth.
> Daniel 2:29–35 (NLT)

THE HEAD OF GOLD

According to Daniel 2, the statue or idol, with its head of gold,
chest and arms of silver, belly and thighs of bronze, and legs of iron
and feet of iron and clay, which Nebuchadnezzar saw in his dream,
represented four great world empires that would arise in world
history, beginning with the kingdom of Babylon. A fifth kingdom
is symbolized in the king's dream as a rock that strikes the idol on its
feet, destroying it. This rock symbolizes a future global superpower
whose dominion will one day cover the entire planet for eternity.

Daniel told the king, "You are the head of gold" (Daniel 2:38 NLT). During his day and throughout history, Babylon became closely synonymous with the reign of King Nebuchadnezzar. Historians have noted that it is appropriate to identify Nebuchadnezzar with Babylon since he was the one who vastly expanded the city architecturally during his forty-three-year reign.[12] The metal used to symbolize the kingdom of Babylon in Nebuchadnezzar's dream is also very appropriate. Gold was a very popular metal in ancient Babylon, so much so that many believe that Babylon is worthy to be called the capital of the golden age of civilization. Upon his visit to Babylon, Herodotus was amazed at the city's lavish use of gold in its imposing sanctuaries that were dedicated to gods such as Bel-Marduk.[13]

THE CHEST AND ARMS OF SILVER

As Daniel continues to explain the dream to King Nebuchadnezzar, he tells him, "After your kingdom comes to an end, another great kingdom, inferior to yours, will rise to take your place" (Daniel 2:39 NLT). We know from world history that the kingdom that succeeded the Neo-Babylonian kingdom was the Medo-Persian Empire. This kingdom is symbolized in the king's dream as the chest and arms of the idol made of silver.

On the night of October 12, 539 BC, the soldiers of Cyrus the Great, also known in history as Cyrus II of Persia, marched into the city of Babylon with little resistance from the Babylonian army, and the city fell into Medo-Persian hands. How the fall happened is a fascinating story.

History and archaeology bear record that at the time before Babylon's fall, King Belshazzar, the grandson of Nebuchadnezzar, was a coregent with his father, King Nabonidus, who for many years had been absent from Babylon, living in Tema of Arabia. Nabonidus wrote that he had "entrusted the kingship to him [Belshazzar]"[14] during his time away from Babylon. It appears that after his long absence from Babylon, Nabonidus had returned to the city to help stave off an imminent attack by King Cyrus of Persia.

To better defend the city and its precincts, Nabonidus divided the Babylonian army into two divisions. One division, commanded by his son Belshazzar, was assigned to fortify the city of Babylon and defend it to the last. Nabonidus then took the remaining Babylonian forces and went out to engage Cyrus in battle several miles from the city. However, things did not turn out as planned.[15]

Herodotus records that "the Babylonians marched out and awaited him, and when Cyrus drew near the city, they joined battle with him. They were defeated, however, and forced to retire within the city walls."[16] Meanwhile, King Belshazzar, oblivious to his father's misfortunes, threw a citywide celebration in Babylon. The prophet Daniel, then an old man in his late eighties, was an eyewitness to Babylon's demise and wrote that on the night that Babylon fell, "King Belshazzar gave a great feast for one thousand of his nobles and drank wine with them" (Daniel 5:1 NLT).

Belshazzar and the Babylonians knew that their city was under siege by King Cyrus, but they were so confident in their fortifications and supplies that they went about the business of partying! Herodotus confirmed Daniel's account when he wrote that on the night that Babylon fell, the Babylonians were engaged in a festival of dancing and reveling[17] and that because the Babylonians "had watched him [Cyrus] attack and conquer so many other nations, they had prepared in advance for a siege by stockpiling enough food to last them many years. For this reason, they were not at all concerned by the siege."[18]

Cyrus knew of the claim that Babylon was an impenetrable fortress. For a time, he was perplexed about how he would make any progress in his siege. The fortifications of Babylon were state of the art, unlike anything Cyrus would have encountered before. The Euphrates River ran through the center of the city so Cyrus came up with a brilliant engineering plan. He decided to divert much of the river's waters farther upstream into a river basin via a canal that he had his army corps of engineers dig. The result? The river farther downstream was significantly lowered to "about midway up a man's thigh."[19] With that accomplished, Cyrus's soldiers, who had been prepositioned for this "drying up" of the river, were able to slip through Babylon's outer and inner defensive walls by wading through the shallow waters of the Euphrates that flowed into the city.

But there was another challenge for Cyrus and his men. The city's defensive wall system also ran alongside the river, and this system had a series of gates. The only way to gain access to the city would have been to open one of these well-secured gates. There is still much speculation today as to just how Cyrus's soldiers were able to breach this river defense system. Many believe that the answer lies in this remarkable prophecy written by the biblical prophet Isaiah, who lived in the eighth century BC. Regarding the fall of Babylon, he wrote,

> This is what the Lord says to Cyrus, His anointed one, whose right hand He will empower. Before him, mighty kings will be paralyzed with fear. Their fortress gates will be opened, never gain to shut against him. This is what the Lord says: "I will go before you, Cyrus, and level the mountains. I will smash down gates of bronze and cut through bars of iron. And I will give you treasures hidden in the darkness—secret treasures. I will do this so you will know that I am the Lord, the God of Israel, the one who calls you by name. (Isaiah 45:1–3 NLT)

Perhaps what is most remarkable about this prophecy is that it mentions Cyrus by name about a hundred and fifty years before he was born! Calling Cyrus His "anointed one," Daniel's God predicted that Cyrus would eventually be the king who would allow the Jewish exiles in Babylon to return to Jerusalem to rebuild their city and temple that had been decimated by the Babylonians.

According to Isaiah's prophecy, Daniel's God came to Cyrus's aid so that the conqueror would carry out His plans to free His people who were in Babylon. The prophecy mentions that Daniel's God would go before Cyrus to "smash down gates of bronze and cut through bars of iron." Hence, Daniel records that "very night Belshazzar, the Babylonian king, was killed. And Darius the Mede took over the kingdom at the age of sixty-two" (Daniel 5:30–31 NLT).

As he continued to interpret the king's dream, Daniel informed Nebuchadnezzar that the kingdom arising after Babylon would be inferior to it (Daniel 2:39 NLT). The head of the idol, which represented the Neo-Babylonian Empire, is made of gold (Daniel 2:32 NLT); in contrast, the chest and arms of the idol, which represents Medo-Persia, is composed of silver. From antiquity to today, silver has been universally accepted as an inferior metal to gold. It is noteworthy that the standard monetary value of the Persians at the time was silver.

THE BELLY AND THIGHS OF BRONZE

Next, Daniel tells King Nebuchadnezzar, "After that kingdom [Medo-Persia] has fallen, yet a third great kingdom, represented by the bronze belly and thighs, will rise to rule the world" (Daniel 2:39 NLT). In the year 331 BC, one of the greatest military battles of the ancient world, a turning point in world history, was fought near the village of Gaugamela in present-day Iraq. Darius III, the last king of the Medo-Persian Empire, had amassed a huge army of about 200,000 men in order to crush the aspirations of the boy king, Alexander the Great. The brilliant Greco-Macedonian king, who had never lost a battle, was on a quest to conquer the entire world. Alexander's Greco-Macedonian armies had swept rapidly through Phoenicia, Palestine, and Egypt and were on a collision course with Darius III at Gaugamela.

As the Greek and Medo-Persian soldiers came head-to-head for one final encounter, "the bronze armor of the Greek soldiers sharply contrasted with the simple woven gowns worn by the Median and Persian soldiers."[19] The Greeks were noted in the ancient world for their extensive use of bronze and used it in their armor, helmets, shields, and weapons.[20] Employing brilliant tactical maneuvers and with the aid of only about 50,000 well-trained Greek soldiers clad in shiny bronze armor, Alexander the Great won a decisive victory at the Battle of Gaugamela that led to the fall of the Medo-Persian Empire.

And so it was that the third great kingdom, represented by the bronze belly and thighs of the idol, which King Nebuchadnezzar saw in his dream, was fulfilled by Alexander the Great and the Greek Empire. After defeating the Medo-Persians at Gaugamela, Alexander pushed east and made it as far as the Indus Valley in India before his soldiers begged him to turn back. He eventually died at the age of thirty-two in the city of Babylon.

THE LEGS OF IRON

Daniel next tells King Nebuchadnezzar, "Following that kingdom, there will be a fourth one, as strong as iron. That kingdom will smash and crush all previous empires, just as iron smashes and crushes everything it strikes" (Daniel 2:40 NLT). Without a doubt, the fourth kingdom is the Roman Empire.

In his eighteenth-century historical treatise *The Decline and Fall of the Roman Empire*, Edward Gibbon strikingly summarized the rise of the Roman Empire this way: "The arms of the republic, sometimes vanquished in battle, always victorious in war, advanced with rapid steps to the Euphrates, the Danube, the Rhine, and the Ocean; and the images of gold or silver, or brass that might serve to represent the nations and their kings were successively broken by the iron monarchy of Rome."[22] Nebuchadnezzar's dream mentions that the fourth kingdom would be "as strong as iron." One commentator notes that the secret to the success and longevity of Rome for nearly five hundred years was found in its "iron army and its iron grip in leadership issues."[23]

In its thirst for conquest, the highly effective Roman military machine smashed and crushed anyone or anything that stood in its way. At its height of power, the empire had conquered and subjugated peoples of varied religions, cultures, and ethnic backgrounds. The fourth kingdom's voracious appetite for conquest is reflected in this statement made by Julius Caesar, who arguably was Rome's most renowned military commander and emperor. "Veni, vidi, vici," meaning, "I came, I saw, I vanquished."[24]

THE FEET OF IRON AND CLAY

Daniel further explains to King Nebuchadnezzar,

> The feet and toes you saw were a combination of iron and baked clay, showing that this kingdom will be divided. Like iron mixed with clay, it will have some of the strength of iron. But while some parts of it will be as strong as iron, other parts will be as weak as clay. This mixture of iron and clay also shows that these kingdoms will try to strengthen themselves by forming alliances with each other through intermarriage. But they will not hold together, just as iron and clay do not mix. (Daniel 2:41–43 NLT)

Rome eventually came to be divided into a western empire and an eastern empire, which is probably symbolized in Daniel 2:33 by the two iron legs of the idol. However, Daniel more explicitly points out in his explanation of Nebuchadnezzar's prophetic dream, "The feet and toes you saw were a combination of iron and baked clay, showing that this kingdom [Rome] will be divided" (Daniel 2:41 NIV). Though the kingdoms of Babylon, Medo-Persia, and Greece were all replaced by a new emerging world empire, over time, the Roman Empire became divided and simply crumbled from within. After succumbing to decades of persistent onslaught by the Germanic peoples from northern Europe known as the Barbarians, the city of Rome fell in AD 476. By the early Middle Ages, these ten prominent Germanic tribes, whose number strikingly corresponds to the ten toes of the idol Nebuchadnezzar saw in his dream— the Alamanni (Germans), Burgundians (Swiss), Franks (French), Lombards (Italians), Saxons (English), Suevi (Portuguese), and Visigoths (Spanish)—had settled all over Western Europe, absorbing all that had once constituted the Roman Empire. Three other tribes, the Heruli, Vandals, and Ostrogoths, are now extinct.

Daniel explained to Nebuchadnezzar that while "some parts of it [the divided Roman Empire] will be as strong as iron, others will be as weak as clay" (Daniel 2:42 NLT). As they settled in western Europe, these Germanic tribes, which eventually came to form the modern nation-states we know today as Germany, Switzerland, France, Italy, the United Kingdom, Portugal, and Spain, along with other European nations, retained much of the Roman legacy in their institutions and culture. Hence, it could be argued that the Roman Empire still exists today, albeit in a divided form. Bible scholar Jacques Doukhan writes that "the passage [Daniel 2] regards that the iron and clay as distinct entities. Iron is to strength as clay is to weakness. The kingdom [Roman Empire], now divided, becomes a heterogeneous composition of weak and strong elements. The territory of the former Roman Empire is a collection of both strong and weak, rich and poor nations."[25]

Daniel also tells Nebuchadnezzar that where he saw in his dream that the feet of the image were mixed with iron and clay, "this mixture of iron and clay also shows that these kingdoms will try to strengthen themselves by forming alliances with each other through intermarriage. But they will not hold together, just as iron and clay do not mix" (Daniel 2:43 NLT). This portion of the prophecy has been an ongoing continuum in European history to the present day. It is a standing joke in Europe that all of its royal families are somehow related. History often bears that out. In a bid to strengthen their kingdoms and political alliances, the royal families of Europe maintained a persistent policy of intermarriage.

Leaders, such as Charlemagne, Napoleon, and Hitler, have also attempted to unite the continent, but to no avail. As he retreated from his eastern campaign into Russia, his army devastated by the Russian winter, Napoleon is reported to have complained, "God Almighty was too much for me." Hitler dreamed that his Third Reich would last a thousand years; it collapsed after only twelve.

Over the centuries, the European nations that came to occupy the territory once held by the Roman Empire also expanded their dominion when they colonized much of the newly discovered lands of the New World. Indeed, today, many of the independent nations that now constitute the United Nations, including the United States of America, were themselves once colonies of the great European powers and, as such, carry with them vestiges of the Roman legacy.

Since the end of the Second World War, the European powers have greatly intensified their efforts to create a United States of Europe, the European Union, an economic, military, and political union on the continent that would be in some form a revival of the Roman Empire. To date, the Achilles' heel of such a union could very well be that the continent is composed of both weak and strong independent nation-states. According to the prophecy of Daniel 2, a united Europe will, ultimately, not succeed "as iron and clay do not mix" (Daniel 2:43 NLT).

THE NEXT SUPERPOWER

Daniel goes on to tell Nebuchadnezzar,

> During the reigns of those kings, the God of heaven will set up a kingdom that will never be destroyed or conquered. It will crush all these kingdoms into nothingness, and it will stand forever. That is the meaning of the rock cut from the mountain, though not by human hands, that crushed to pieces the statue of iron, bronze, clay, silver, and gold. The great God was showing the king what will happen in the future. The dream is true, and its meaning is certain. (Daniel 2:44–45 NLT)

What world power today is represented by the fifth kingdom described in the verses above? Are these verses describing the future dominance of a rising Chinese superpower? Do they foretell a future in which a singular godlike artificial intelligence entity emerges on the world stage and creates a "perfect" global civilization in order to control every aspect of human life? If we examine the prophecy of Daniel 2 carefully, it is quite evident that the fifth kingdom cannot represent a rising Chinese superpower because this kingdom literally enters human reality overnight and erases all traces of every human civilization that came before (Daniel 2:34–35). Not even our Chinese friends, as industrious as they are, would be able to accomplish should a remarkable feat.

The prophecy of Daniel 2 is clear. It is the God of heaven, Daniel's God, who sets up the fifth and final world kingdom that is still in the future (Daniel 2:44–45). Daniel's prophecy reveals that this future kingdom will never be destroyed or conquered by another nation; it will last forever. Upon its establishment, this future world superpower will remove every trace of all other world empires that have come before (Daniel 2:35).

Whereas in his dream, Nebuchadnezzar sees the first four kingdoms symbolized in the statue by the metals gold, silver, bronze, and iron—metals often associated with manmade idols—this fifth kingdom is represented by a stone that eventually grows into a huge mountain. In the Bible, a stone in its brute form is typically used to represent the divine dimension, God and the Messiah.[26]

It is in this fifth and final kingdom, the kingdom of God, that humanity will at long last have true happiness, peace, prosperity, and eternal life. In God's coming kingdom, there will be no more death, sorrow, pain, or crying because, in the new heavens and new earth, all traces of these things would have passed away (Revelation 21:4). As we trace the prophetic timeline outlined in the image of Daniel 2 right down to its toes, what becomes strikingly apparent is that we are now living in a period in history in which the next expected major event is the establishment of this fifth and final global kingdom.

Jacques Doukhan observes,

> None of the statue's kingdoms are very important—they serve only as landmarks leading to the last prophecy concerning the divine kingdom. They act as chronological markers, situating God's coming kingdom in time. The statue's four kingdoms teach us two things about God's kingdom: first, it is real and will actually manifest itself in history, just as the human kingdoms did. Second, the data of the prophecy allow us to conclude that we are in the time of the end, close to its appearance.[27]

Ultimately, Daniel was right on all the kingdoms so far—even those that came many years after him. Any reason then not to trust him on the last kingdom, the fifth and final one?

CHAPTER 3

GLIMPSES OF GOD

The famous twentieth-century British philosopher and Nobel laureate Bertrand Russell was once asked under what condition would he believe in God. Russell replied, "Well, if I heard a voice from heaven and it predicted a series of things which came to pass, then I'd have to believe there's some kind of supernatural being."[1] For me, perhaps the most stunning aspect of the book of Daniel is that it confronts us with the profound reality that the God of the Bible, a supernatural, super-intelligent being who transcends humanity, really exists. William Shea writes that "to propose that someone, utilizing only natural human resources, could correctly predict what was going to happen five, six, or seven centuries in advance, as in the case of the book of Daniel, goes far beyond any natural human knowledge. Such insight could only have come only from the realm of the supernatural."[2]

As Daniel reveals King Nebuchadnezzar's dream and its interpretation, he says, "There are no wise men, enchanters, magicians, or fortune tellers who can reveal the king's secret. But there is a God in heaven who reveals secrets, and he has shown King Nebuchadnezzar what will happen in the future" (Daniel 2:27–28 NLT). In the book of Isaiah, Daniel's God declares that He is the only being in the universe capable of opening for us the mysteries of the future with remarkable accuracy. He states, "Remember the things I have done in the past. For I alone am God! I am God, and there is none like me. Only I can tell you the future before it even happens. Everything I plan will come to pass, for I do whatever I wish" (Isaiah 46:9–10 NLT).

With such powerful biblical evidence for God's existence, it is imperative that we seriously consider what God is saying to us about Himself, our life, and our world. As we listen, we will find answers to important questions and catch many wonderful glimpses of God that will change our lives. I used to think that if God exists, then why doesn't He just call a press conference and reveal Himself to the world? What is with all the hiding? If God is real and all-powerful, why does He allow pain and suffering? Why doesn't God just snap His fingers and make things right? These are reasonable questions, and in this chapter, I will begin to share some of the amazing things that I have personally discovered in their answers.

What does God want from us? God is ultimately trying to communicate to us that He has something much better planned for humanity than this life is offering. God is aware of the challenges that you and I face daily in our broken, dysfunctional world. He wants us to come into His presence one day and see Him face-to-face (1 John 3:2). And herein lies the most incredible reason why God is trying to get our attention. God is extending to us the opportunity of a lifetime. He is offering us the gift of eternal life. God wants us to spend eternity with Him if we choose to accept His gift.

God, I have personally discovered, is not a distant, alien, and uncaring being. He is a relational being who yearns to have a relationship with every human being. God says to us, "I know the thoughts that I think toward you ... thoughts of peace and not of evil, to give you a future and a hope ... you will seek Me and find Me, when you search for Me with all your heart" (Jeremiah 29:11–13 NKJV).

So how do we make contact with God? Scripture reveals that "anyone who wants to come to Him must believe that God exists and that He rewards those who sincerely seek Him" (Hebrews 11:6

NLT). In other words, a belief or realization that God exists and that He is able to guide you through the unseen realities of your relationship with Him is the first step on a journey to discover more about God.

Theoretical physicist John Polkinghorne shares that there is an odd view today that faith involves shutting one's eyes and believing impossible things because an unquestionable authority says you should. He writes that "the leap of faith is a leap into the light and not into the dark. It involves a commitment to what we understand in order that we may learn and understand more ... you will never see anything if you don't stick your neck out a bit ... we shall never have God neatly packaged up. He will always exceed our expectations and prove Himself to be a God of surprises. There is always more to learn."[3]

THE HEAVENS DECLARE
THE GLORY OF GOD

Growing up in a mountainous area in Jamaica, at night I would often go out into our backyard to stare at the night sky for hours. An amateur astronomer, I would imagine what existed beyond the stars that I could see and what was beyond all that I could not see. I would often try to fathom what the edge of the universe might look like and even try to count the stars. The immensity of the universe often boggled my mind. The astronomer Claudius Ptolemy, who lived in the second century BC, estimated that there were as many as 1,022 stars. Today, we know that a single star seen with the unaided eye from the earth is quite possibly a cluster of several spiraling galaxies, each containing billions of stars! Our own disk-shaped spiraling Milky Way galaxy contains about 100 million stars. Jason Lisle, an astrophysicist, observes that "not only did God make the universe beautiful, He made it unimaginably large."[4]

The psalmist David wrote that "the heavens proclaim the

glory of God. The skies display his craftsmanship" (Psalm 19:1 NLT). Every time we admire the glories of the night sky, we are, in fact, catching a glimpse of God's greatness, His love of beauty, His wisdom, His power, and His majesty (1 Chronicles 29). The same super-intelligent being who reveals the mysteries of the future also created the universe and fixed the stars in place. Through the prophet Isaiah, God declares, "To whom will you compare me? Who is my equal?" … Look up into the heavens. Who created all the stars? He [God] brings them out like an army, one after another, calling each by name. Because of His great power and incomparable strength, not a single one is missing" (Isaiah 40:25–26 NLT).

Lisle adds that "the more we 'magnify' the universe, the more we are amazed by its beauty and complexity. The same is true for the Creator of the universe. The more we magnify God, the more we realize just how amazing He is. It seems that God has constructed the universe to reflect this aspect of His character."[5] It is important though for us to understand that God is not the universe; He is its Creator. Even as His presence pervades every sector of the cosmos, God is not limited or confined to the universe but transcends it (Psalm 139:7–9). King Solomon, said to be the smartest man who ever lived, affirms that "the highest heavens" cannot contain God (1 Kings 8:27 NLT).

For decades, scientists have theorized that of all the planets in our solar system that could be made more earthlike, Mars seems to be the most promising candidate. First, Mars lies in a region of our solar system where water can remain liquid. Also, while an earth day is about 23.9 hours, the length of a Martian day is comparable at about 24.62 hours. Though the Martian atmosphere is primarily composed of carbon dioxide, scientists theorize that oxygen could be added to the atmosphere if plants were cultivated on the planet's surface using a process of photosynthesis. We have also learned in recent times that there is an abundance of water trapped in a subterranean lake near Mars's south pole. In theory, a massive project to make Mars more earthlike would take decades or even centuries to complete before the Red Planet would be deemed habitable.

When it comes to Mars's next-door neighbor, however, the Bible reveals that God made the earth, our Blue Planet, to be inhabited (Isaiah 45:18). There is no biblical evidence that God used violent random evolutionary processes that played out over billions of years to create life on earth. Genesis, the biblical book of beginnings, reveals that God used six literal twenty-four-hour days to accomplish His creative acts on earth and that He "merely spoke," and all life on the planet came into existence. The Genesis creation account outlines a logical and orderly sequence that demonstrates that God is a planetary engineer par excellence.

A survey of Genesis reveals that God used the first four days of creation to make the earth habitable for human and animal life. The book records that on the first day of creation, God calls for light and also sets in place earth's twenty-four-hour day and night rotation cycle (Genesis 1:3–5). On day two of creation, God sets the planet's breathable atmosphere in place (Genesis 1:6–8). On day three, He created living space on the planet for both man and beast and caused the earth to bring forth plant life (Genesis 1:9–13). On day four, God fine-tuned the heavenly bodies to serve for "signs to mark off the seasons, the days, and the years" (Genesis 1:14–19). After He made the planet habitable, God proceeded on the fifth day to create all marine life and birds of every species (Genesis 1:20–23). Finally, His work of creation culminated on the sixth day with the creation of the land animals and, with his crowning act of creation, humankind—male and female—who were made in His image.

GOD IS LOVE

As a child, I was terrified of God. The onset of a torrential, tropical downpour saw me scurrying under the nearest bed to avoid being zapped by the lightning of God. I was petrified of God's wrath because I reasoned that if Santa Claus knew that I had been naughty and not nice, then surely God would have also been aware of my sullied life. Many people hold similar views of God. For them, God is like an angry father, a vengeful being who takes delight and almost fiendish pleasure in punishing us for our misdeeds.

The truth is God's character has been maligned by a long-running smear campaign that has persisted throughout the ages. Thus, we must rely on the Bible alone to give us trustworthy and reliable glimpses of God's character. I was to discover in later years that from Genesis to Revelation, the Bible consistently testifies of a loving God who is compassionate, gracious, merciful, just, forgiving, and slow to anger (Exodus 34:6–7; Jonah 4:2; James 5:11). In fact, the Bible declares that God is love (1 John 4:7).

The ancient Greeks often employed four words to connote the meaning of "love," namely *philia, eros, storge,* and *agape*. According to the Greeks, *philia*, from which we get the name Philadelphia, describes a love that is rooted in the loyalty and tender affection we have for friends and community. *Eros*, or erotic love, describes the passionate, sensual love a man and woman have for each other. *Storge* love describes the natural affection a parent has for a child, and *agape* love is love in its purest deepest form—love that is unconditional and self-sacrificial.

The Bible often uses the Greek word *agape* to describe God's love for humanity. God's agape love manifests itself in acts of kindness. It is "self-giving, other-directed love,"[6] a love that, the apostle Paul writes, "cares more for others than for self" (1 Corinthians 13 MSG). The deepest natural affection that we have for those nearest and dearest to us falls way short of this divine agape love because our love is often tainted with selfishness.

The Bible affirms that God is love and that love is the defining trait of His essence and character. Scripture reveals that even as there is one God, the Godhead is composed of a community of three persons, Father, Son, and Holy Spirit—three divine beings who love and care for each other. Each person within this divine community also delights in glorifying each other (John 16:13–15; John 17:1–5; Hebrews 1:1–12).

Scripture not only reveals that God is love but also that His love reaches out in a divine embrace to all of His creation. Because of His love for His creatures, God has chosen to locate His sanctuary, His dwelling place, within the confines of His created universe so that He can have communion with His creatures (1 Kings 8:49; Psalm 102:19; Psalm 103:19). This does not take away from the reality that His presence inundates all spheres of the universe (Psalm 139:7–10).

From His heavenly sanctuary, the command center of the universe, God presides over all activities in the cosmos. His right to rulership and worship by the intelligent universe is founded on the reality that He is the Creator and Sustainer of all (Revelation 4:11). The foundation of His throne is His law of love, and this law enjoins all creatures to love their Creator with all their being and to love their neighbor as themselves (Exodus 20:1–17; Matthew 22:37–40).

As God's intelligent creatures, we are not like robots that are preprogrammed to carry out the instructions of their creator. Instead, as beings created by God with the capacity to love, we have been given free will, free choice. After all, how could anyone be forced to love? It's a contradiction in terms. When we then, using this sacred gift of free will, choose to live in harmony with God's law of love, we are choosing to align ourselves with God's will for us that ultimately brings us into everlasting happiness. On the other hand, if we choose to rebel against God's love, we are choosing to separate ourselves from the Source of our being. Consequently, we are placing ourselves in danger of being eternally separated from God.

The incredibly good news is that God has never given up on us or stopped loving us! God yearns for us to live in harmony with Him. His love for us remains unchanged, perfect, and unconditional. God assures us, "Can a woman forget her nursing child, and not have compassion on the son of her womb? Surely they may forget, yet I will not forget you" (Isaiah 49:15 NKJV). Even though we are tainted and blighted with selfishness, God still yearns for His agape love to fill our lives so that we will be perfect in Him (1 John 4).

COSMIC CONFLICT

Clearly, as we look around us, we can see that there is something fundamentally wrong with our world. We are reminded daily of horrific crimes, pandemics, climate change, wars, and civil unrest, leading some to wonder if our civilization is fast approaching its tipping point. The global wars of the twentieth century stand out for their mass devastation and for their demonstration of man's inhumanity to man. Millions were mercilessly exterminated on the fields of battle and in gas chambers and crematoriums. Images of mass graves littered with thousands of naked, skeletal human forms are forever seared in our collective human consciousness.

If God is good, if God is love, if God is all-powerful, why does He allow such terrible atrocities? If God is just, fair, and gracious, why does He allow the evil of racial discrimination to continue? If everything that God made in the universe was good and perfect, then where did evil come from? Why does God allow the poor and the less fortunate to suffer?

Journalist Lee Strobel writes that on a trip to Bombay, India, he came face-to-face with a scrawny and malnourished Indian child, the sight of whom stopped him in his tracks. One of the boy's eyes was diseased and half-closed. His hair was matted with dirt; he had blood oozing from scabs on his face. As the boy extended his hands to beg coins, Strobel wondered, "If God had the power, why didn't He show up in that festering Indian hell hole slum in order to heal and rescue that child?"[7]

The Bible does, in fact, pull back a cosmic curtain to provide us with some answers to these questions, and what it reveals is that our planet is embroiled in an ongoing cosmic conflict between good and evil. We see this cosmic conflict been played out daily among the nations in their never-ending quest for supremacy and domination. We see the conflict raging daily in our cities, neighborhoods, homes, and own lives. The good news is that scripture reveals that, in the end, good triumphs over evil. God is not at all responsible for the pain, suffering, and death so endemic in our world. There is something else at play here.

WAR IN HEAVEN

When we think of heaven, we think of the place in the universe where the Creator has made His dwelling place among His creatures. We think of a place where love, joy, peace, and happiness reign supreme. We think of an everlasting blissful existence.

Yet the Bible discloses that there was a time when war broke out in heaven. The apostle John writes, "There was war in heaven. Michael and his angels fought against the dragon and his angels. And the dragon lost the battle, and he and his angels were forced out of heaven. This great dragon—the ancient serpent called the devil, or Satan, the one deceiving the whole world—was thrown down to the earth with all his angels" (Revelation 12:7–9 NLT).

A war in heaven? How could this have happened in God's perfect universe? According to Revelation, this conflict in heaven was centered around two main characters, Michael and the dragon. Who is Michael? Who is the dragon? And what were they warring about?

The name Michael, or its Hebrew derivative, *Miyka'el,* literally means, "Who is like God." Jewish tradition and many Bible scholars have held for centuries that Michael was the archangel or chief angelic being who fought the dragon on behalf of the Creator in the war that broke out in heaven. However, we have several reasons to believe that Michael is another name for the Son of God. For now, we will focus on unmasking the identity of the dragon because, as it turns out, this being was primarily responsible for the conflict which arose in heaven.

We are plainly told that the dragon is "the ancient serpent called the devil, or Satan" (Revelation 12:9 NLT). Many people, even some Christians, do not believe in the devil. Popular culture tells us that the devil is a mythical, red-skinned monster with goat's horns and hoofed feet who wields an iron pitchfork and lives in an inferno in the underworld.

The Bible reveals, however, that the devil is a real being who plays a prominent role in the cosmic drama that is presently engulfing our world. Scripture reveals that the devil is a master deceiver. Perhaps his greatest deception is that he has managed to convince much of the world that he does not exist! Still, obvious questions remain. How did the devil get into God's perfect paradise, and why did a loving God, the Creator of all things visible and invisible, create a devil?

The Bible is clear that everything that God created was perfect and good (Genesis 1:31; 1 John 1:5). We are told that there is no trace of evil in the Creator (Psalm 92:15). Scripture does reveal that, at some point, however, God created a perfect angelic creature named Lucifer, who eventually chose to rebel against his Creator and became the devil, or Satan. In Greek, the word often used for devil is *diabolos,* which can be translated as slanderer or accuser. Similarly, the Hebrew word used for Satan is *ha-Satan,* which means adversary or prosecutor.

Writing about Lucifer's eventual downfall, the prophet Isaiah states,

> How you are fallen from heaven, O Lucifer, son of
> the morning! How you are cut down to the ground,
> you who weakened the nations! For you have said
> in your heart; I will ascend into heaven, I will exalt
> my throne above the stars of God; I will also sit
> on the mount of the congregation on the farthest

sides of the north; I will ascend above the heights of the clouds, I will be like the Most High. (Isaiah 14:12–14 NKJV)

Adding to Lucifer's biography, the prophet Ezekiel writes,

You were the seal of perfection, full of wisdom and perfect beauty. You were in Eden, the garden of God; Every precious stone was your covering: the sardius, topaz, and diamond, beryl, onyx, and jasper, sapphire, turquoise, and emerald with gold. The workmanship of your timbrels and pipes was prepared for you on the day you were created. You were the anointed cherub who covers; I established you; you were on the holy mountain of God; you walk back on forth in the midst of the fiery stones. You were perfect in your ways from the day you were created, till iniquity was found in you. (Ezekiel 28:12–14 NKJV)

From these insights, we know that before he became Satan, the adversary and the accuser of his brethren, the devil was a beautiful and powerful angel in heaven named Lucifer. The name *Lucifer* literally means *light-bringing* and probably meant that Lucifer was once one of God's prime angelic messengers in the universe. He is described as being the "anointed cherub who covers" or "the anointed cherub with overshadowing [wings]" who was stationed on "the holy mountain of God" or the utmost heights of heaven. This probably meant that he was one of the most exalted and most powerful of all of God's creatures, as his position in heaven literally placed him next to the throne of God.

When he came from his Creator's hand, Lucifer's character was unblemished. There was no trace of evil in this perfect angelic creature. Ezekiel writes, "You were the seal of perfection, full of wisdom and perfect beauty ... you were perfect in your ways from the day you were created, till iniquity was found in you" (Ezekiel 28:12–14 NKJV). Over time, however, Lucifer's thoughts became self-centered, and gradually something strange and mysterious began to take shape in his heart that turned him into the devil. The prophets write,

> Your heart [Lucifer's] was lifted up because of your beauty; you corrupted your wisdom for the sake of your splendor. (Ezekiel 28:17 NKJV)

> You have said in your heart; I will ascend into heaven, I will exalt my throne above the stars of God ... I will ascend above the heights of the clouds, I will be like the Most High. (Isaiah 14:13–14 NKJV)

Somehow, because of his beauty, power, and exalted position in heaven, Lucifer corrupted his wisdom by cherishing the foolish thought that perhaps he could be like God. Perhaps he reasoned that if he could attain a higher position in heaven, he would then receive the homage and worship of angels and thereby become equal with the Most High God. Ezekiel adds that "by the abundance of your trading you became filled with violence within, and you sinned" (Ezekiel 28:16 NKJV). The word "trading" here is not used in the commercial sense as in the trading of goods and services but refers to the campaign Lucifer launched in heaven in a deliberate attempt to maliciously smear God's character.

His heart filled with malice, envy, and covetousness, Lucifer became a slanderer and accuser of the Most High and thus became Satan. Like a crafty yet foolish politician, he may have reasoned that if he could rally all the angels in heaven to his side, he could demand that God make certain changes to His government. Over time, he must have projected a vision of his own self ambitions in the hearts and minds of many of the angels, deceiving them into believing that God was restricting their advancement to a higher plane of existence.

It appears that Lucifer had tremendous influence over the angelic heavenly host because he was able to convince one-third of them to join him in his rebellion against God (Revelation 12:3–4). John, the revelator, writes, "War broke out in heaven" (Revelation 12:7 NKJV). Lucifer's war of ideas gradually manifested itself into active revolt, and it was determined that he and his fellow rebels could no longer stay in heaven. "The great dragon was cast out, that serpent of old, called the Devil and Satan, who deceives the whole world; he was cast to the earth, and his angels were cast out with him" (Revelation 12:9 NKJV).

FALLEN

Humans became caught up in the cosmic conflict when Satan brought his rebellion to our planet. Genesis reveals that after the creation of life on planet earth, the first man and woman, Adam and Eve, were placed in a lush, beautiful garden named Eden. This Edenic paradise that once bloomed on the earth supplied everything that the human pair and their posterity would ever need. A pure, unpolluted river ran through the garden. Eden was filled with a myriad of luxuriant, fragrant flowers; lush, beautiful greenery; and several varieties of fruit trees that were "pleasant to the sight and good for food" (Genesis 2:9 NKJV).

God instructed the first man and woman to "fill the earth and govern it" (Genesis 1:28 NLT). As the designated representatives of earth in God's vast creation, Adam and Eve were assigned the task of caring for the planet and its creatures. At the center of Eden, God planted two special fruit trees. One of these trees was the tree of life. It was God's intent from the beginning that Adam and Eve, along with their descendants, would eat from this tree of life and live forever. Most likely, as humans regularly partook of the fruit from this tree of life, their bodies would be reinvigorated. They would never grow old, feeble, or sick. They would forever retain their youthful vitality and have an endless existence. The other tree that was placed at the center of Eden was the tree of the knowledge of good and evil.

God commanded the human pair, "You may freely eat the fruit of every tree in the garden—except the tree of the knowledge of good and evil. If you eat its fruit, you are sure to die" (Genesis 2:16–17 NLT). When God created humankind, He gave us the gift of free will. This means that as conscious, thinking, sentient beings, we are free to choose a course of action. In light of the war that had broken out in heaven, God placed the tree of the knowledge of good and evil in Eden to serve as a simple moral test of humanity's loyalty to Him.

The choice before Adam and Eve was simple. If they chose to obey God, then they would be destined to spend a blissful eternal existence with Him; if they disregarded His instructions, then humanity's lot in life would be alienation from God. From the beginning, Satan plotted the eternal ruin of humanity, so he showed up in Eden and became maliciously obsessed with orchestrating the downfall of the human pair. It is, unfortunately, quite evident that Adam and Eve chose to listen to his lying words instead of obeying the words of God (Genesis 3).

But why didn't God just snap His fingers and destroy Lucifer when he rebelled? Why did God allow this rebel to continue to run wild? Part of the answer must be that God is merciful and takes no pleasure in the destruction of the wicked (Ezekiel 18:30–32). In all probability, God made several appeals to Lucifer and his rebellious party. Also, it stands to reason that if God had immediately destroyed the rebellious angels, many of the unfallen beings would have then proceeded to worship Him out of fear rather than love. Therefore, to secure the eternal well-being of the universe, the Creator decided that He needed to give the devil and his rebellious party time so that all would eventually come to see the disastrous consequences of their rebellion.

The consequences of Adam and Eve's disobedience have been tragic, disastrous, and devastating for the human race. All evil in this world can be traced back to that fateful choice that the first human couple made in Eden. In addition to losing their Eden home (Genesis 3:22–24), the first human couple was also barred from the tree of life. The result is that death is now the fate of humanity. We all find that sooner or later, death sneaks up on us, scythe in hand, and snatches us away in his deadly grip.

Even though medical advances and healthy lifestyle choices continue to extend our life span, over time, our youthful vitality diminishes. We become old, feeble, sick, and finally, we die. None of us really wants to die. This is because God has planted eternity in the human heart (Ecclesiastes 3:11). As our body eventually settles down for the long sleep of death, a message instinctively screams out to every cell in our being from the very core of our DNA that says to us that death is an anomaly, that it is unnatural, for we were meant to live forever.

God designed that Eden would serve as His special meeting place on earth where He would commune with humanity. Before their fall, Adam and Eve had often enjoyed intimate face-to-face encounters with God. They had often looked forward to the Creator's timely visits to Eden, joyfully praising and adoring Him as He revealed His glorious presence to them. After their rebellion, instead of happily rushing out to meet Him when He called out to them, they ran and hid from God. This has been the story of the human race ever since.

Instead of reaching out to God, we often turn our backs to Him. Often when we hear God calling out to us, we try to convince ourselves that maybe if we just ignore His calls long enough, He will eventually give up and go away. We try to convince ourselves that, perhaps, if we deny God's existence, the still, small voice we often hear in our heart will be silenced forever. But as we try to press on in a cruel, unforgiving world, we eventually discover that there is a gaping hole in our heart that family, relationships, career, success, money, sex, drugs, or fame cannot fill. This emptiness in our heart can only be filled by a relationship with God.

SLAVES TO SIN

The truth about our human condition is that we are all slaves to sin. New Testament evangelist Paul writes, "For everyone has sinned; we all fall short of God's glorious standard" (Romans 3:23 NLT). The human dilemma is that everyone born into this world (except for one) has sinned. All of us have fallen short of God's glorious moral standard. The Bible is clear that a rebellious life of sin leads to death or eternal separation from God. Further lamenting the human predicament, Paul adds that "no one is righteous—not even one. No one is truly wise; no one is seeking God. All have turned away; all have become useless. No one does good, not a single one" (Romans 3:10–12 NLT).

Even though none of us share the guilt of Adam's original sin (Ezekiel 18:20), the moment we are born into this fallen world, there are tremendous impossible odds stacked against us. As Adam's descendants, we all carry within our veins DNA that has been ravaged and weakened by centuries of human rebellion. All of us have inherited human frailties from our parents, and as such, we all have an overpowering propensity for rebellion against God's will.

Just about now, you may be saying to yourself, "What in the world is this guy saying? I can't be all that bad! Compared to all the wretched banes of society, I am a fairly decent, moral, good, law-abiding, and upstanding citizen!"

Yet when we honestly compare ourselves to God's glorious moral standard or His law of love (Exodus 20:1–17), our life falls glaringly short of what God expects of us (Romans 3:19). The Bible is clear that "everyone who sins is breaking God's law, for all sin is contrary to the law of God" (1 John 3:4 NLT). In his book *To Know*

God, author Morris Venden writes that "sin ... is living a life apart from God, and it makes no difference how good a life that might be. There are many people who live good, moral lives apart from God. But they are living in sin. Their good lives are sin."[8] That is because when we live outside a relationship with God, our motives for doing good will always be tainted by our own selfishness and self-centeredness. Put another way, people who truly do not know God will many times do the right things for the wrong reasons.

The reality is that we can never by our own good deeds make ourselves right with God. The prophet Isaiah says, "We are constant sinners; how can people like us be saved? We are all infected and impure with sin. When we display our righteous deeds, they are nothing but filthy rags. Like autumn leaves, we wither and fall, and our sins sweep us away like the wind" (Isaiah 64:5–6 NLT). As slaves to sin, we are trapped in a vicious, deadly cycle. As we emerge from the dense smokescreen of lies that so often engulfs our existence, the truth that confronts us is that, as fallen beings, we stand as condemned criminals on death row before the universe.

We are helpless to help ourselves. Left to ourselves, we are doomed to suffering, misery, disappointment, pain, and death. Like Paul, as we come to grips with our fearful condition, we cry out, "Oh, what a miserable person I am! Who will free me from this life that is dominated by sin and death?" (Romans 7:24 NLT). But there is hope. Because of His boundless love and mercy, God has not abandoned us to utter despair and eternal loss. He has devised and activated a divine plan in which we can find redemption. It is known as the Gospel.

CHAPTER 4

NO GREATER LOVE

God's response to humanity's suffering, pain, and death was to come down into it Himself. He could not bear the thought that our rebellion would eternally separate us from Him. Out of their love for us, the Godhead—the Father, the Son, and the Holy Spirit—gave up one of their members, the Son of God, for the redemption of humanity. Scripture reveals that "God so loved the world that he gave his one and only Son, that whoever believes in him shall not perish but have eternal life" (John 3:16 NIV).

That God would give up His only Son is the most amazing development in the history of the universe. That the Creator of the universe, the Son of God, "whose goings forth are from old, from everlasting" (Micah 5:2 NKJV), would stoop to become human, to become one of us, to become Immanuel, God with us, boggles the mind.

Scripture reveals that "when the right time came, God sent forth His Son, born of a woman ... to buy freedom for us ... so that He could adopt us as His very own children" (Galatians 4:4 NLT). Hundreds of years before the Son of God came to our world, God, through His holy prophets, gave us certain signs, or messianic prophecies in scripture, that would help us to pinpoint the time of His Son's arrival. The time prophecies of Daniel 9 have been called "the crown jewel of the Old Testament" because they pinpoint, about five hundred years before He was born, the very year when the Son of God would begin His ministry on earth and also the year of His death. The startling accuracy of these time prophecies caught the attention of Sir Isaac Newton, who called them "the foundation stone of the Christian religion."[1]

Based on prophecy in Daniel 9:25–27, we know that the Son of God, the Christ or Messiah, would begin His earthly ministry in the second decade of the first century AD. Only one person in history fulfilled all the messianic prophecies in scripture. That person was and is Jesus of Nazareth. Born to a carpenter named Joseph and his fiancée, Mary, in the Judean town of Bethlehem (Luke 2:1–7), the Creator, Jesus, instead of choosing the palatial home of an earthly potentate, humbled Himself, made Himself of no reputation, and was born to poor peasants in a barn with a manger for a crib.

For the first thirty years of His earthly life, Jesus lived in obscurity as a lowly carpenter in Nazareth, a Galilean town of ill repute. In biblical times, Nazareth was a small, unimportant village in the backwoods of Galilee that was not even close to any of the frequently traveled routes in Israel. Its population was under five hundred; it had a poor reputation among the Jews for laxity in morals and religion. People living there were generally despised by the Jews and even by the Romans.[2] It is no wonder then that Nathaniel, who later became a disciple of Christ, wondered aloud if anything thing good could come out of Nazareth (John 1:46). Jesus did indeed come out of Nazareth—untainted by His unsavory surroundings!

YOU ARE MY WITNESSES THAT I AM GOD

The year is AD 27, and the nation of Israel is a stir with a patriotic excitement that borders on national hysteria and revolution. Israeli zealots frequently organize themselves into resistance groups and launch skirmishes against the strongholds of their Roman occupiers.

Rome's response is to viciously clamp down on these Jewish dissenters. Hundreds of Jewish freedom fighters are cruelly executed for their rebellious actions against the Empire. However, Rome's frequent brutal retaliation does nothing to dampen a Jewish enthusiasm for independence that is fueled by visions of messianic deliverance.

It was in this expectant atmosphere that the greatest of the messianic prophets, John the Baptist, began to preach. His message was simple. "Repent for the kingdom of heaven is at hand" (Matthew 3:2 NKJV). Thousands of Jews flocked to the wilderness of Judea to hear John as his message of the coming kingdom of God resonated with the national mood. At the center of the Baptist's message was the imminent coming of the Messiah, and all Jews wanted to have a part in the new era that was about to dawn in Israel's history.

It is not by happenstance that the Jews have been so consequential in world history. It is true that Israel has been blessed as a people. Yet they were not chosen by God because of their race, intellect, or any unique qualities that they innately possessed. Israel was blessed as a nation because of the faithfulness of their ancestor Abraham. Early in their history, Moses reminded the Hebrews, "The Lord did not choose you and lavish His love on you because you were larger or greater than other nations, for you were the smallest of all nations! It is simply because the Lord loves you, and because He was keeping His oath he had sworn to your ancestors" (Deuteronomy 7:7 NLT).

When God called the patriarch Abram (who was later renamed Abraham) to leave Ur of the Chaldeans to go to Canaan, the patriarch demonstrated unquestioning obedience to God to such an extent that the Bible calls him "the friend of God" (James 2:23 NLT) and "the father of all those who believe" (Romans 4:11 NKJV).

God had called Abraham in order to bequeath to him and his descendants the everlasting salvation promise that He made to Adam and Eve in Eden (Genesis 3:15). God's plan is to save humanity and to restore righteousness, mercy, and justice to our planet. It was His design that the descendants of Abraham would be a holy people, His "own special treasure from among all the nations of the earth ... a kingdom of priests, [His] holy nation" (Exodus 19:5–6 NLT), who would demonstrate in their lives an example of how God expects all of humanity to live. When we quickly trace the history of the descendants of Abraham, Isaac (Abraham's son), and Jacob (Abraham's grandson), we actually see God putting into action His great salvation plan to save humanity. In His divine providence, God geographically placed Israel at the ancient crossroads of the nations so that all the nations of the earth would naturally come in contact with them.

It was God's design that the seed of the woman, Jesus Christ, the one who would destroy the serpent and save humanity, would be born in Israel. This was the reason for this promise made to Abraham: "In your Seed [Jesus] all the nations of the earth shall be blessed" (Genesis 22:18 NKJV). It is Jesus Christ, the root of David, who will one day establish God's kingdom of justice and righteousness on earth (Jeremiah 23:1–8). It was also God's plan that Israel would serve as His witness in all the earth that He exists as the Creator and Redeemer of humankind.

Speaking through the prophet Isaiah, God declared,

> Gather the nations together ... can any of them predict something even a single day in advance? Where are the witnesses of such predictions? Who can verify that they spoke truth? But you are my witnesses, O Israel ... and you are my servant. You have been chosen to know me, believe in me, and understand that I alone am God. There is no other God; there never has been and never will be. I am the Lord, and there is no other Savior ... you are witnesses that I am the only God ... from eternity to eternity I am God. No one can oppose what I do. No one can reverse my actions. (Isaiah 43:9–13 NLT)

Israel's special status in the world as God's holy people was contingent upon their remaining faithful to the Creator. God instructed them, "If you will obey me and keep my covenant, you will be my own special treasure from among all the peoples on earth; for all the earth belongs to me" (Exodus 19:5 NLT). History reveals that over time, Israel broke their covenant relationship with God. As a nation, they lost their way so that by the time Jesus of Nazareth appeared in their midst, they had very misguided notions of what the Messiah would do.

HEALING IN HIS WINGS

As John the Baptist preached in Israel about the coming Messiah, Jesus of Nazareth also went to the Jordan River to be baptized by him. As He emerged from the water, God the Father and the Holy Spirit publicly recognized Jesus as His Son and testified that He had lived a blameless life (Matthew 3:16–17). Immediately after His baptism, Jesus went into the Judean wilderness for forty days and forty nights to prepare for His public ministry. While He was there, the devil accosted him and made several tempting propositions that were designed to distract and dissuade Him from His mission to rescue humanity (Matthew 4:1–11).

Falsely styling himself as an angel of enlightenment (2 Corinthians 11:14), the malevolent pied piper has made it his mission to deceive and darken the minds of billions. Forever banished from heaven, Lucifer, along with his unseen demonic agents, has ensnared the human race in a cosmic web of rebellion and turned our world into a cesspool of evil. Having turned our backs on our Creator, we have all become slaves to Satan's evil empire.

The Bible calls the devil "the prince of the power of the air, the spirit who works in the sons of disobedience" (Ephesians 2:2 NKJV). Satan has nothing but hatred for the human race and is bent on destroying us. This powerful fallen angel, along with his millions of other enraged demons, often employs all of his powers to cause floods, fires, tornadoes, hurricanes, and earthquakes for the destruction of humanity. The result is that a choking smog of evil now hovers over our suffering planet.

We have become the spectacle of the unfallen universe as our world is now the main arena in the great cosmic drama. The contenders in the cosmic conflict are seeking to win the allegiance and devotion of every human heart. Jesus came to our planet to disarm the powers of darkness and destroy the works of the devil (Colossians 2:15; 1 John 3:8). He came to our world in order to wrest the dominions of this world from the evil one. He came to seek and to save that which was lost (Luke 19:10). Where Adam had yielded to temptation and sinned, Jesus overcame the devil at every step.

Filled with God's love and passionate commitment to healing humanity, Jesus traveled across the towns and villages of ancient Israel, announcing God's kingdom and healing people of all their sickness and disease (Matthew 9:35). Humbling Himself and taking the form of a servant, the Son of Righteousness descended into our blighted world to rescue us from certain death.

As vast crowds reached out to Him for healing, Jesus had compassion on them and cured them. The consensus was that "everything He does is wonderful. He even makes the deaf to hear and gives speech to those who cannot speak" (Mark 7:36 NLT). Not only did Jesus cure the infirm of their ailments, but He also extended God's hand of grace in order to restore them to righteousness. In a wonderful way, Jesus's ministry of healing and restoration gives us a glimpse of God's glorious future kingdom in which there will be no more disease, pain, heartache, or death because the Great Physician, the Son of God, will ever be with us.

Jesus drove out the demons who had long tormented the people. With the power and authority of the Son of God, He declared to the masses, "If I am casting out demons by the Spirit of God, then the kingdom of God has arrived among you. For who is powerful enough to enter the house of a strong man like Satan and plunder his goods? Only someone even stronger—someone who could tie him up and then plunder his house" (Matthew 12:28–29 NLT). Jesus's coming had inaugurated the promise of a new beginning for the human family. Truly, the Son of Righteousness had arisen on our dark world with healing in His wings.

NO GREATER LOVE

Among those who were drawn by the words and deeds of the humble Galilean teacher and healer was the Pharisee Nicodemus. As a member of the Sanhedrin, the Jewish national council, Nicodemus was a highly educated Pharisee with membership in one of the most conservative and exclusive first-century Jewish religious sects. As teachers of the law, they heavily promoted the idea that it was only through their good works that Israel would be able to retain the favor of God for the preservation of their nation and the establishment of God's kingdom. During His ministry on earth, Jesus publicly denounced the Pharisees' hypocrisy and pointedly exposed the burdensome, nonsensical religious traditions that these leaders had placed squarely on the people. As a result, Jesus was constantly at odds with these Jewish leaders.

Despite all of his pride and prejudices, Nicodemus must have felt strangely drawn to Jesus. He had, most likely, prided himself that his place in the kingdom of God was secure because of his many good works and strict adherence to the Torah and the traditions of the elders. Yet as he listened to the words of Jesus of Nazareth and witnessed His many miraculous healings, he must have thought something was missing. Many questions surely stirred in his mind. Was Jesus indeed Israel's long-sought Messiah? Were the Jews about to enter an age of eternal glory with the overthrow of Roman tyranny and the establishment of God's kingdom in Israel?

The proud Pharisee decided to seek Jesus for a private night interview. As he came into Jesus's presence, Nicodemus, we can imagine, felt strangely awed and apprehensive. Striving to maintain his composure, he began the interview with a measured cadence intended to convey an air of dignity and authority. "Rabbi," he began, "we all know that God has sent you to teach us. Your miraculous signs are evidence that God is with you" (John 3:2 NLT). Jesus lovingly examined the man before Him, instantly read His life's story, and immediately prescribed the dire need of his soul. "I tell you the truth," Jesus said solemnly, "unless you are born again, you cannot see the kingdom of God" (John 3:3 NLT).

What did Jesus mean that Nicodemus needed to be "born again"? The Greek word for *born* is *gennao*, which means "to be born" or "to be conceived." The Greek word *anothen* is translated in some Bibles as "again" but literally means "from above" or "from a higher place." Therefore, Jesus was telling Nicodemus and us that if we desire to inherit eternal life, we must experience the new birth that comes from the Creator God above.

As creatures made in the image of God, we have been damaged by our constant rebellion against God's will. By pointing out our need to be born again, Jesus is simply saying that the only way for us to reflect the fullness of God's character is to submit ourselves to a work of re-creation that God accomplishes in us through His Son, Jesus Christ.

His mind stymied by unbelief, Nicodemus listened with incredulous amazement as Jesus unfolded the mysteries of God's plan to save humanity. He wondered aloud how these things could even be possible. Jesus assured Nicodemus that humanity's redemption becomes a possibility because of His impending sacrificial death for the sins of humanity, to which Jesus alluded.

Separated from God, we find ourselves in a fearful predicament because a death penalty hangs over our heads as a result of our rebellious attitude and behavior. Scripture reveals the good news that "God demonstrates His own love towards us, in that while we were still sinners, Christ died for us" (Romans 5:8 NKJV). To liberate us from this death penalty, the Son of God volunteered to die for our sins. By dying on the cross for us, Jesus took the death penalty for our sins upon Himself.

This amazing demonstration of God's love for us had been foreshadowed for centuries in the animal sacrifices of the Jewish Old Testament sanctuary. These sanctuary rituals were, in fact, compacted prophecies that pointed to the one great sacrifice that Jesus made as the Lamb of God who takes away the sins of the world. In the divine counsels of heaven, the Son of God told the Father, "You did not want animal sacrifices or sin offerings. But you have given me a body to offer ... Then I said, 'Look, I have come to do your will, O God, as it is written about Me in the Scriptures'" (Hebrews 10:5–7 NLT).

In order that He could die for us, the Son of God, by His own volition, took on our humanity, which He will retain forever. Though He is fully God (Colossians 2:9), by His own free will and out of His love for us, Christ also became fully man. The author of Hebrews writes, "Because God's children are human beings—made of flesh and blood—the Son also became flesh and blood. For only as a human being could He die, and only by dying could He break the power of the devil, who had the power of death. Only in this way could He set free all who have lived their lives as slaves ... Therefore, it was necessary for Him to be made in every respect like us" (Hebrews 2:14–17 NLT).

As His three-and-a-half-year ministry on the dusty roads of Palestine came to an end, "Jesus resolutely set out for Jerusalem" (Luke 9:51 NLT), for it was there that His rescue mission to save humanity was to culminate on the cross. Over time, many of the Jews had become disenchanted with Him because, even though He had demonstrated through His miraculous healing power and wonderful words that He was the Messiah, He had refused to use His power to lead them in an insurrection against Rome in order to establish an age of worldly glory for Israel. Adding to this, the Jewish leaders had become jealous and concerned with Jesus's growing popularity and influence among the people. They reasoned that He had to be executed if Israel's special relationship with Rome was to be maintained for the preservation of the nation (John 11:45–51).

Unjustly condemned, Jesus was turned over to the Roman authorities to be executed by crucifixion. Roman crucifixion was a terrible and gruesome ordeal. Unlike the quick heart-stopping surge of an electric chair or the fast, deadly, corrosive poison of a lethal injection, crucifixion was intended to be a slow and torturous execution. Designed by the Romans to humiliate their victims, the condemned criminals were stripped, stretched out on the wooden cross, and then impaled with seven-inch rusty iron nails through their wrists and ankles, which would have crushed the median nerve in their hands, causing intolerable pain.[4] After the cross was hoisted violently into place, there were cases where victims lingered on the instrument of torture for days. Hundreds of years before the crucifixion of Jesus, the prophet Isaiah described in prophetic prose the horrible ordeal Jesus would endure for us.

> He was pierced for our rebellion, crushed for our sins. He was beaten so that we could be whole. He was whipped so that we could be healed ... He was led like a lamb to the slaughter. And as a sheep is silent before the shearers, He did not open His mouth ... but He was struck down for the rebellion of my people ... He was counted among the rebels. He bore the sins of many. (Isaiah 53:7–8 NLT)

Jesus died within hours after being nailed to the cross, something that was rare among crucifixion victims. He probably died of a broken heart because of the sheer mental agony brought on by our sin (Luke 22:39–44; John 19:33–34). After He had laid down His life for us, three days later, He took it up again.

RISEN SAVIOR

Today the most wonderful news that has echoed and reverberated throughout the corridors of history is that Jesus of Nazareth has risen from the dead! Jesus is alive! The one who was crucified for us more than two thousand years ago is alive, and He holds tomorrow in His hand. That ancient tomb in Israel where the crucified Savior of the world was once laid is empty because Jesus rose from the dead!

After His crucifixion and burial, Jesus's closest followers hastily retreated to a secret upper room apartment in Jerusalem and hid there out of fear. Earlier, when they had gone to the Garden of Gethsemane with Jesus to pray, they had all forsaken Him when the Jewish authorities showed up to arrest Him. Later that morning when identified publicly as one of Jesus's followers, Peter, with much cursing and swearing, denied any connection with the condemned Nazarene. During Jesus's darkest hour on earth when He was persecuted and slaughtered by the Romans, His closest friends and followers turned out to be unbelieving cowards.

Yet just fifty short days later in the face of threats of imprisonment, torture, and death for believing in the risen Nazarene, this same Peter, along with the other disciples, boldly proclaimed to all of Jerusalem and the world that Jesus of Nazareth had risen from the dead.

What happened to the disciples that caused such a radical shift in their outlook and disposition? The most logical and credible explanation for their behavior is that they had seen the resurrected Jesus, as they claimed. What else could have caused such a dramatic and complete change?

New Testament expert Gary Habermas notes that the resurrection of Jesus was "the central proclamation of the early church from the very beginning. The earliest Christians didn't just endorse Jesus's teachings; they were convinced they had seen him alive after his crucifixion."[1] Because they had seen their risen Lord, the first-century disciples were willing to die for what they knew to be true, and many of them did. Jesus had told His disciples that though they would experience great sorrow and disappointment, their sorrow would be turned into great joy. "Now is your time of grief, but I will see you again and you will rejoice, and no one will take away your joy" (John 16:22 NIV). Believers should never allow anyone to take away the great hope and joy they have in their risen Savior.

Why is it important for Christians today to have the assurance that Jesus is alive? The answer is that the resurrected Jesus is the Christian's guarantee that if he or she dies believing in Christ, he or she will be raised from the dead to eternal life at the Second Coming of Jesus (John 6:40; John 11:25; 1 Corinthians 15:20–23; 1 Thessalonians 4:16–17). If it had turned out that Christians worship a dead Messiah, then following Jesus of Nazareth would have been the greatest hoax of all time, a pointless and futile exercise. Paul the apostle, himself a former skeptic and persecutor of the early Christian church, writing to the believers at Corinth, argued, "If Christ has not been raised, then your faith is useless, and you are still guilty of your sins. In that case, all who have died believing in Christ are lost! And if our hope in Christ is only for this life, we are more to be pitied than anyone in the world" (1 Corinthians 15:17–19 NLT).

INVITATION TO AN ABUNDANT LIFE

Today Jesus is asking us a vitally important question that He had asked His disciples centuries ago. "Who do you say I am?" (Luke 9:20 NLT). Do you believe that I was a wonder-working healer, an astute philosopher, or just a special man who transformed history? Do you believe that I am the Son of God who died for your sins?

If you want to take the first steps on a journey that leads to eternal life, then you must *believe* that Jesus is the Son of God. Then by faith, you must accept His sacrifice of death on the cross for your sins.

After witnessing God's miraculous deliverance of the apostle Paul and his companion Silas from a dungeon prison, a trembling Macedonian jailer asked the men of God, "Sirs, what must I do to be saved?" The reply that came was simple. "Believe in the Lord Jesus and you will be saved" (Acts 16:30–31 NLT).

Believing in Jesus involves placing all of our trust, our hopes, and our confidence in Him as Savior. The Bible invites us to behold the Lamb of God who takes away the sins of the world. Without question, the cross of Calvary demonstrates God's matchless unconditional commitment to fallen humanity. Scripture attests that "there is no greater love" (John 15:13 NLT) than what was demonstrated by God at Golgotha in Jerusalem over two thousand years ago. By taking the penalty for our sins upon Himself, Christ has opened the door for us to spend eternity with Him because He "tasted death for everyone" (Hebrews 2:9 NLT) and offers everyone a new life in Him.

In order for Jesus to transform us, to give us a new life in Him, we must repent of our sins. Repentance is genuine sorrow for a life of rebellion against God, and it is accompanied by a decision to turn away from that lifestyle. It is confessing and admitting to God that we have done wrong and that we have rebelled against God's divine will. Genuine repentance, therefore, involves prayerfully and fervently reaching out to God and humbly inviting Him to create within us the right impulses and attitudes so that our entire life will be pleasing to Him.

Perhaps the most famous example of genuine heartfelt repentance recorded in scripture is the prayer King David prayed after he had committed adultery with Bathsheba and murdered her husband, Uriah. As he cried out to God, David exclaimed,

> Have mercy on me, O God, because of your unfailing love. Because of your great compassion, blot out the stain of my sins. For I recognize my rebellion; it haunts me day and night. Against you,

and you alone, have I sinned; I have done what is
evil in your sight ... purify me from my sins, and
I will be clean; wash me, and I will be whiter than
snow ... remove the stain of my guilt ... create
in me a clean heart, O God. Renew a right spirit
within me. (Psalm 51:1–10 NLT)

In order for us to become new creatures in Christ, we too need
to experience the type of repentance that David had. Perhaps your
life story so far has been even worse than David's! The good news
is that it does not matter what you have done. God is able to mold
you into a new creature. Nothing you have done—no matter how
evil, heinous, ugly, or degrading—could ever place you beyond the
reach of God's love, grace, and forgiveness, except your own refusal
to accept what Christ offers you. The amazing thing is that God's
perfect love for you remains unconditional even if others in your life
have written you off!

Scripture says that "if we confess our sins to him, he is faithful
and just to forgive us our sins and to cleanse us from all wickedness"
(1 John 1:9 NLT). In other words, if you go to God in faith, sincerely
repenting and confessing your sins, in that very moment, He forgives
you. God is able to remove your sins from you as far as the east is
from the west and will cast them into a sea of forgetfulness (Psalm
103:11–12; Micah 7:19). God's promise to all who truly repent of
their sin is this: "I will forgive their wickedness, and I will never
again remember their sins" (Hebrews 8:12 NLT). God tells us that
"he who covers his sins will not prosper, but whoever confesses and
forsakes them will have mercy" (Proverbs 28:13 NKJV).

In the new birth, we are not only saved by the death of Christ
but also by the life of Christ (Romans 5:10). What does that mean?
Well, it means that at the very moment that we repent and confess
our sins to God, Jesus not only forgives us and cleanses us from all
our filthiness and unrighteousness, but He also covers us with the
robe of His righteousness with His own perfect life. God's perfect

moral law of love demands a life of perfect goodness. This we do not have to give because our lives have fallen woefully short of God's perfect standard (Romans 3:23).

While on earth, Jesus lived a sinless life, meaning "He condemned sin in the flesh" (Romans 8:3 NKJV). In other words, He overcame sin as a human being, so "that the righteous [and just] requirement of the Law might be fulfilled in us" (Romans 8:4 NKJV). In other words, Jesus overcame all the temptations and never once sinned! Never once did he rebel against the will of His Father. He is the only human being who has ever lived a perfect life.

When we choose to become willing participants of God's grace, Christ credits the record of His perfect life of goodness to our own record so that as we stand before God and the universe, we are declared not guilty because not only has Christ died for us, but He has also credited His own life of goodness to our record!

No wonder the apostle Paul declared, "There is no condemnation for those who belong to Christ Jesus" (Romans 8:1 NLT). Isaiah adds, "I will greatly rejoice in the Lord, my soul shall be joyful in my God; for He has clothed me with the garments of salvation, He has covered me with the robe of righteousness" (Isaiah 61:10 NKJV).

Repentance is a gift from God. Amazingly, scripture also declares that it is the goodness of God that leads us to repentance (Acts 5:30–31; 2 Timothy 2:25). Left to our own devices, we would never see the need to turn to God. Christ passionately declared, "And I, if I am lifted up from the earth, will draw all peoples to Myself" (John 12:32 NKJV). As One who is deeply in love with us, He is always trying to woo us to Himself because He really wants us to spend eternity with Him.

As in a love letter to us, you can almost hear Jesus pleading,

> Why will you die? Return to Me, and I will return to you. I love you so much. I know exactly what you are going through in your life right now. I can feel your pain because I have walked in your shoes.

I am coming back to this planet soon to gather the citizens of My kingdom, and I want you to be ready to join Me when I return. I want you to have eternal life so that you and I can spend eternity together.

Come to Me now just as you are. Don't put it off. Don't worry about your past. If you return to me, I will forgive you for all your mistakes. I will make a personal request to My Father, in the presence of the righteous angels in heaven, that you spend eternity with Me and will erase every record of your misdeeds that are recorded in the books of heaven. These are my promises to you. Please put your trust in Me and accept my gift of salvation.

Do you hear Jesus's voice speaking to your heart? Why don't you reach out to Him in faith right where you are and confess your sins? The truth is that we never need a human priest or a pastor to connect with God. We are told that we have "a great High Priest who has entered heaven, Jesus the Son of God ... so let us come boldly to the throne of our gracious God. There we will receive His mercy, and we will find grace to help us when we need it most" (Hebrews 4:14–16 NLT).

FOLLOW ME

What does it mean to follow Jesus today? Does following Him mean that we become committed members of a church community? Yes, joining a community of like-minded believers is a central part of God's salvation plan. The Greek word used for "church" in the New Testament is *ekklesia*, which simply means "the called-out ones." Hence, God's church on earth represents a community of believers who have chosen to take a stand with Jesus by following Him wherever He leads them.

Billy Graham said that "following Christ ... means we seek to obey Him every day. He knows what is best for us and has told us how He wants us to live in His Word, the Bible."[2] Ultimately, following Jesus involves a personal decision on our part to live daily by every word that comes from God in scripture so that Jesus will be the Savior and Lord of our lives. John 14:15 says that following Jesus means that if we love Him, we will heed His commandments and have an abundant life (John 14:15). Jesus tells us, "If anyone desires to come after Me, let Him deny himself, take up his cross daily and follow Me" (Luke 9:23 NKJV). Here Jesus is telling us that following Him involves self-denial and cross-bearing.

Denying oneself means that our earthly self-interests become secondary to the interests of Jesus and the kingdom of God. When Christ is truly Lord and Master of your life, you will honor Him above all others. You will not have divided loyalties. You will not idolize others above Him. Your relationship with Him will take first priority above everything thing else, including that of your spouse, children, parents, extended family, country, political affiliation, career, finance, favorite sports team, music, or Hollywood celebrity.

Jesus says to us, "If you love your father or mother more than you love me, you are not worthy of being mine; or if you love your son or daughter more than me, you are not worthy of being mine. If you refuse to take up your cross and follow me, you are not worthy of being mine" (Matthew 10:37–39 NLT).

When we remind ourselves that Jesus is not only humanity's Savior but that He is also our Creator God, then the claim that He makes on your life and mine does not seem unreasonable! The first and greatest commandment in the Bible tells us that we should love God with all our heart, mind, and soul (Matthew 22:37–38). John the apostle tells us that "we know what real love is because Jesus gave up His life for us" (1 John 3:16 NLT). It is only as God takes first place in our heart that we truly begin to understand what it means to love our spouse, our children, our parents, and all who are dearest to us.

When we think of the cross and Jesus's suffering, persecution and death come to mind. Yet when Jesus asks us to take up our own cross if we are to follow Him, what does He mean (Luke 9:23)? Jesus explains in the Gospel of John that "the world would love you as one of its own if you belonged to it, but you are no longer part of the world. I chose you out of the world, so it hates you ... a slave is not greater than its master. Since they persecuted me, naturally they will persecute you" (John 15:19–20 NLT). So what is Jesus saying here? It's simple. As we forge a genuine relationship with Him and choose to follow Him, our characters become radically transformed in Christ, and we naturally come into conflict with a fallen world whose spirit is contrary to Christ. The result could well be conflict—a tension that arises even in our own household.

The apostle Paul writes that "everyone who wants to live a godly life in Christ Jesus will suffer persecution" (2 Timothy 3:12 NLT). The Greek word for "persecute" in the New Testament is *dioko,* which means to pursue or attack. Don't be surprised or alarmed if your life becomes radically unsettled when you pledge to follow Jesus. Most often, you will lose old friends and gain new ones. Satan often tries to turn his malice on God's people in a bid to discourage them, destroy them, and disqualify them for heaven. Rest in the assurance that Jesus stands guard over your life and that in the end, none of the devil's attacks will stand (Isaiah 54:17; Ephesians 6:10–18).

When we compare the cost of following Jesus to the eternal rewards that God promises us, all the suffering, trials, and tribulations will all pale by comparison. Paul writes that "what we suffer now is nothing compared to the glory He will reveal to us later" (Romans 8:18 NLT). The eternal rewards that Christ will bestow on His faithful followers who overcome the trials of this life are literally out of this world!

CHAPTER 5

THE MAN WHO
HOLDS TOMORROW

Mention the word *Revelation,* and people think of the antichrist, the mark of the beast, Armageddon, and the end of the world. For many, the last book of the Bible is but a ghastly blueprint of the future, a harrowing apocalyptic doomsday scenario depicting humanity's worse fears and nightmares. Yet the book of Revelation was not written to stoke our worst fears and phobias but to prophetically delineate our brightest hopes and dreams.

This book of destiny reveals that, at present, we stand on the threshold of a wonderful eternal existence in which God will make all things new. Revelation tells us that there will be no more death, sorrow, crying, or pain because God Himself will wipe away every tear from our eyes. Revelation assures us that despite all the evil we see in the world, God will soon intervene and establish a new order of things.

Yet surprisingly, despite the incredibly good news contained in the book and the glorious hopeful future that it unveils, Revelation is often ignored even by Christians because it employs visions and symbolic imagery. Many have struggled to decipher its meaning. In his book *Future Glory*, Revelation expert Angel Rodriquez writes,

Some biblical writers used stories or narrated the way the Lord led his people in the past in order to strengthen the faith of their contemporaries (e.g., 1, 2 Kings). Others communicated their messages through sermons in the form of poetry (e.g., Isaiah 40–66), songs (e.g., psalms), wisdom sayings (e.g., Proverbs), or letters (e.g., Romans). Daniel and Revelation stand apart from those in the complexity of the images and language used to receive and communicate the divine revelation. [1]

And so, because of the relative complexity of its literary style, many have assumed that Revelation's prophetic message remains sealed or closed. Yet this assumption flies in the face of the opening chapter of the book that tells us, "God blesses the one who reads the words of this prophecy to the church, and He blesses all who listen to its message and obey what it says, for the time is near" (Revelation 1:3 NLT). In other words, it was God's intention from the first century when the church began that all would read the book of Revelation and heed its message. This verse says that God blesses anyone who reads it.

Still, if it is God's intention that all would understand the messages of Revelation, why did He employ such extensive use of symbolic language and imagery in its prophecies?

For starters, by employing verbal, visual, and other types of symbols, God was essentially communicating to us in human language. Rodriquez adds that "symbols surround us, and we use them almost unconsciously. The Lord was using a human structure of communication in order to reach us with His message." [2] And so, like the dramatic images in a movie, the visual symbolic language in Revelation piques our interest.

However, employing daily news headlines or nefarious sensationalist content from web sites in order to decode Revelation could prove detrimental. With so many misleading ideas and interpretations about Revelation, how do we correctly decipher the book?

First, we need to understand that John's symbols were drawn from the first, not the twenty-first century. Because they have attempted to use twenty-first-century imagery to decipher first-century symbols, many contemporary readers of Revelation have formulated "dangerous speculations and unsound personal opinions."[3] Revelation outlines the history and experiences of Christians from the first century until the future Second Coming of Jesus. Even though it does allude to certain nations and powers, Revelation should not be used as a prophetic treatise of secular human history or current events (Revelation 1:1).

We should always allow the Bible to interpret itself. Revelation expert Ranko Stefanovic writes that "most of the symbolism of the book [of Revelation] is taken from the Old Testament—some three-fourths of the book's text has direct or indirect allusions to the Old Testament. In portraying future events, inspiration often uses the language of the past."[4] Therefore, I will often refer to Old Testament passages. The book of Revelation is not a revelation of beasts, wars, plagues, or dragons but a revelation of Jesus Christ (Revelation 1:1). Jesus is the preeminent figure in the book.

REVELATIONS FROM PATMOS

About the year AD 94, a prisoner on the small rocky Greek island of Patmos in the Aegean Sea, the apostle John, was given a vision of Jesus, who showed him "events that must soon take place" (Revelation 1:1 NLT). These visions became the book of Revelation. Christian tradition holds that the aged apostle had been arrested in Ephesus for preaching the Word of God and for his testimony about Jesus (Revelation 1:9) and then was sent to Rome, where he was cast into a boiling cauldron of oil. After miraculously emerging unscathed, John was banished by the emperor Domitian to Patmos, the Alcatraz of the Roman Empire.

As John tells it, one day while he was filled with the Holy Spirit and engrossed in worship, he heard a loud voice that sounded like a trumpet blast behind him, declaring, "I am the Alpha and the Omega, the First and the Last ... what you see, write in a book and send it to the seven churches which are in Asia" (Revelation 1:11 NKJV). As John turned to see who was speaking, he came face-to-face with a being with eyes that glowed like fire and whose face shone like the brilliance of the noonday sun. The man's head and hair were as white as snow, His feet were like polished brass, and His voice thundered and reverberated like crashing ocean waves. John recognized this majestic celestial being as Jesus, his Lord and Savior; however, he faints out of fear in the presence of his glorified Lord. But Jesus touches and reassures him, "Don't be afraid! I am the First and the Last. I am the living One. I died, but look—I am alive forever and ever! And I hold the keys of death and the grave" (Revelation 1:17–18 NLT).

What wonderful words of assurance! The Lord is reminding us that our hope and our future exist in Him, the Resurrection and the Life, the First and the Last, the One who died for us and is now alive for evermore. The good news from Patmos is that Jesus lives, and He is the only One who has life-giving power over death and the grave! This promise that He made to Martha on the occasion of the resurrection of Lazarus still rings true today. "I am the resurrection and the life. Anyone who believes in me will live, even after dying. Everyone who lives in me and believes in me will never ever die" (John 11:25–26 NLT).

Someone once said that we don't need to be afraid of tomorrow because God is already there. We don't need to be afraid of the future because if we know Jesus intimately, as it is our privilege to know Him, then we can rest in the assurance that one day we will spend a glorious eternal existence with Him in a future already prepared for us.

It has been over two thousand years since Jesus ascended to heaven. But have you ever wondered what Jesus is doing for us in heaven today? When John, through a vision, has an intimate encounter with Jesus on Patmos, he sees Jesus clothed in priestly garments, wearing a golden sash girded around His chest and standing in the middle of seven golden lampstands. These seven lampstands are reminiscent of the menorah that provided light in the Jewish temple. It was the daily job of the priests to trim the lamps and provide them with fresh oil to ensure that they kept burning.[5]

While on earth, Jesus told His disciples that they were the light of the world. Before His ascension, He assured them that He would provide them with the oil of the Holy Spirit so that they would shine as beacons of hope in a world of darkness (Acts 1:8). Therefore, in Revelation, the seven lampstands represent not only actual churches in John's day but also God's church throughout history. It is profoundly revealing and reassuring that John sees Jesus standing in the middle of the seven lampstands, which shows the Savior's closeness, devotion, and concern for His church throughout the ages.

In scripture, the priests had two primary responsibilities. They were to offer sacrifices for the sins of the people and to perform a work of intercession. After He had borne the death penalty for our sins, Jesus ascended to heaven where, as our heavenly High Priest, He initiated a work of intercession for us (Isaiah 54:12; Romans 8:34; Hebrews 8:1–6).

Today we are encouraged to confidently approach God's mercy seat in heaven by faith and prayer so that we can receive help in times of need (Hebrews 4:14–16). We are assured that as we approach God's throne of grace in heaven, admit our wrongs to Jesus, and receive Him as our Lord and Savior, that "He [Jesus] is ... able to save to the uttermost those who come to God through Him, since He always lives to make intercession for them" (Hebrews 7:25 NKJV).

Therefore, as our Intercessor, Jesus applies to the life of the penitent sinner the benefits of salvation that He bought for us with His own blood on Calvary. Today, we can be assured that Jesus hears every prayer, cleanses us from every confessed sin, extends forgiveness to us, credits to us His own perfect life record of right living, and gives us divine power to live holy lives.

THE SCROLL OF HUMAN DESTINY

Early in Revelation, John is transported across space and time to the heavenly temple, the headquarters of the universe. He was conveyed there in a vision in order to witness a significant cosmic event— the enthronement of Jesus as King of the universe after He had ascended to heaven. As he is given a glimpse of the heavenly temple, John sees an expansive sea of glass as clear as crystal stretched out for what seemed like miles, with a majestic throne, high and lifted up, marking its seemingly endless horizon. The throne of God is surrounded by a rainbow of deep radiant hues, and from it issued lightning, the rumblings of thunder, and the sound of many rustled, whispered voices. God the Father, the Ancient of Days, sits on the throne. His presence radiates a brilliant, unapproachable light that illuminates the temple and its occupants. His penetrating gaze surveys all sectors of the cosmos—past, present, and future.

Near to the throne, John sees four powerful angelic beings who, with veiled faces and prostrated forms, worship unceasingly day and night before God with the adoring cry "Holy, holy, holy is the Lord God, the Almighty" (Revelation 4:8 NKJV). Also, standing on the sea of glass before the throne of God is an innumerable company of angels. Yet on this celestial occasion, John notices that the special guests of honor seated nearest to the throne are twenty-four humans who have been redeemed from the earth. All twenty-four representatives from earth are dressed in shining white robes with crowns of gold on their heads. Who are these humans in heaven, and how did they get there? We know from scripture that Enoch, Elijah, and Moses were eventually taken to heaven by God. We also know that when Jesus rose from the dead, many believers were raised with Him (Matthew 27:51–53). The twenty-four humans who John sees in heaven may well have been these believers, including Enoch, Elijah, and Moses (Ephesians 4:8).

As the heavenly inauguration ceremony gets underway, John notices a scroll sealed with seven seals in the right hand of God the Father. An angel steps forward and proclaims with a loud voice, "Who is worthy to open the scroll and to loosen its seal?" (Revelation 5:3 NKJV). There is a momentary pause in heaven, and John begins to weep as there seems to be no one qualified in the universe to open the scroll and loosen its seals. Why was John weeping? What significant information did the scrolls contain?

The scroll appears to have something to do with the overall purpose of the book of Revelation. It likely contains information about the future destiny of the church and the world that John eventually wrote down for our benefit.[6] John is not permitted to weep for long. One of the twenty-four humans redeemed from the earth draws near to him and tells him excitedly, "Stop weeping! Look closely, the Lion of the tribe of Judah, the Root of David, has overcome and conquered! He can open the scroll and its seven seals" (Revelation 5:5 NLT).

John then jumps for joy as he sees his Master and friend, Jesus, approach the brilliant presence of His Father and take the scroll from His right hand. Revelation expert Jon Paulien states that in Revelation, the scroll is symbolic both as a will and as a deed. Roman wills were sealed by six witnesses and the testator. Like a will, the scroll can be opened because the testator Jesus died a sacrificial death for our sins. As a deed of purchase, the scroll represents the title deed of the world that was forfeited when Adam and Eve sinned. By His sinless life and death, Jesus redeems the forfeited inheritance and thus becomes worthy to break the seals and restore rightful ownership.[7]

As the great Conqueror who gained a great victory on the cross for humanity takes the scroll of human destiny in His hands, Jesus— the man who holds tomorrow—is reinstated on the throne of God. His coronation as King of kings and Lord of lords is completed.

Rapturous praise erupts in heaven, affirming that Jesus is the only one worthy to break the seven seals of the scroll to reveal humanity's destiny.

REVELATION'S TIMELINE

One reason why Revelation appears mystifying, and puzzling, is that the book is not organized or structured in the same way that a typical book would be today. Most books in the twenty-first century start out with an introduction, then the body of the book, and finally a conclusion. Not Revelation. When it comes to apocalyptic prophecy, God often uses a literary structure called "recapitulation," in which He will say the same thing more than once, often using different symbols and words and then adding more detail.

Why does God use this literary method? Why not? This is a human way of communicating. Great teachers, authors, and communicators understand the importance of repeating their messages. Therefore, God believes that His message for humanity in Revelation is so vital, so important, that He often repeats His divine prophetic messages and gives us more detail with each repetition.

Outside its prologue (Revelation 1) and its epilogue (Revelation 22:6–21), Revelation is essentially divided into three major sections: the messages to the seven churches (Revelation 2–3:22), the heavenly inauguration scene of Jesus and the seven seals (Revelation 4–11:1–19), and the latter part of the book that gives detailed information about the final events in Christian history (Revelation 12–22:1–5).

Each of these sections traces events that start in John's day, and each ends with descriptions of events at the close of human history. In other words, each section covers the same history and prophecy but from different perspectives. I will use the seven seals as a timeline for Revelation's historical, prophetic events.

THE FIRST SEAL

> Now I saw when the Lamb opened one of the seals; and I heard one of the four living creatures saying with a voice like thunder, "Come and see." And I looked, and behold, a white horse. He who sat on it had a bow; and a crown was given to him, and he went out conquering and to conquer. (Revelation 6:1–2 NKJV)

Unless the text indicates otherwise, we should always assume that the book's chapters and passages are written in symbolic or figurative language. In the first chapter and verse of Revelation, John writes that the book has been "signified" (Revelation 1:1), meaning that the book is written using symbolic code. The Greek word used for signify is *semaino,* which means "to show by signs and symbols."[8]

When Jesus opens the first seal, John sees a rider on a white horse with a bow in his hand going forth to conquer. To decipher this first seal, we first refer to Psalm 45:3–7 (NIV), which reads,

> Gird your sword on your side, you mighty one; clothe yourself with splendor and majesty. In your majesty, ride forth victoriously in the cause of truth, humility and justice; let your right hand achieve awesome deeds. Let your sharp arrows pierce the hearts of the king's enemies; let the nations fall beneath your feet. Your throne, O God, will last forever and ever; a scepter of justice will be the scepter of your kingdom. You love righteousness and hate wickedness; therefore, God, your God, has set you above your companions by anointing you with the oil of joy.

Psalm 45 contains one of many messianic prophecies in the Old Testament. The verses of this messianic prophecy are instructive because they portray the Messiah as a militant leader who rides forth to conquer "in the cause of truth, humility, and justice." The conquests of the Messiah end with a royal wedding with him marrying His bride[9] (Psalm 45:10–15), which most certainly alludes to the coming marriage of Christ and His church (Revelation 19:6–9).

The first seal contains striking allusions to Psalm 45. First, the rider in Psalm 45 goes "forth victoriously in the cause of truth, humility, and justice." In the first seal, the rider of the white horse is going "out conquering and to conquer." In biblical imagery, the symbol of a horse conveys strength and power in battle (Job 39:19; Proverbs 21:31). Also, a white horse conveys the purity, truth, and righteousness of the rider's cause (Daniel 7:9; Revelation 1:12–14; 6:11; 19:8; 19:11; 20:11).

As the rider of the white horse goes out victoriously, the only weapon he carries is a bow. A bow, of course, is useless without arrows. The prophet Isaiah declared, "He made my mouth like a sharpened sword, in the shadow of his hand he hid me; he made me into a polished arrow and concealed me in his quiver" (Isaiah 49:2 NIV). From this, we can infer that the rider of the white horse goes out "conquering and to conquer" with arrows, or powerful words of truth and righteousness, that He proclaims to all.

Who might the rider of the white horse be? Does he represent a false Christ as some believe? The rider of the white horse cannot be the antichrist because the color of his horse (white) reflects the purity of His aims. Also, later in the book of Revelation, we see Jesus figuratively riding a white horse when He returns to triumph over his enemies on earth (Revelation 19:11–16). The mission of Jesus and the rider of the white horse is similar.

In addition, John observes that the rider of the white horse wears a *stephanos*, a crown of victory similar to the garlands given out to participants at ancient Olympic games rather than the royal crown or *diademata* (Revelation 19:12) that Jesus wears. When Paul talks about the crown of righteousness that believers receive at the Second Coming of Jesus, he is talking about the *stephanos*, the crown of victory (2 Timothy 4:8). Interestingly, the woman of Revelation 12 who represents God's people or His church, also wears a crown of victory or *stephanos* (Revelation 12:1). Paulien writes that "it seems best ... to understand the white horse to symbolize Christ's kingdom and its gradual conquest of the world through the preaching of the gospel by His Church. What was ratified in heaven at the enthronement of the Lamb is now actuated in the experience of His people in the course of human history."[10]

Immediately after His inauguration (or enthronement) in heaven, Jesus pours out the Holy Spirit on His disciples; they are now empowered to take the Gospel to the world (Acts 1:8; 2). From Jerusalem, the Gospel spreads to the Jewish diaspora but ultimately finds its greatest conquests among the God-fearing Gentiles of the Roman world. Through the missionary exploits of Paul and others, the church is established in cities like Antioch of Syria, Ephesus, and Rome. By the end of the first century, the church had made significant inroads in just about every major center of the Roman Empire, even encroaching on areas, such as North Africa and Egypt.

The rider of the white horse, therefore, represents the powerful and rapid expansion of the early Christian church throughout the known world in the apostolic age (c. AD 31–100). Jon Paulien adds that "the phrase 'conquering to conquer' expresses a progressive increase of victory [for the Gospel], the white horse does not end with the first century. Rather, the symbol portrays in a general way the progress of the gospel during the entire Christian Era."[11] Indeed, the conquests of the rider of the white horse eventually culminates with the Second Coming of Jesus as King of kings, who Himself figuratively rides forth on a white horse as a great Conqueror in order to subdue His enemies and to establish His eternal kingdom (Revelation 19:11–21).

THE SECOND SEAL

> When He opened the second seal, I heard the second living creature saying, "Come and see." Another horse, fiery red, went out. And it was granted to the one who sat on it to take peace from the earth, and that people should kill one another; and there was given to him a great sword. (Revelation 6:3–4 NKJV)

Who or what is represented by this second horseman? In the Gospel of Matthew, Jesus gives us an important clue. He states, "Do not think that I came to bring peace on earth. I did not come to bring peace but a sword. For I have come to set a man against his father, a daughter against her mother, and a daughter-in-law against her mother-in-law; and a man's enemies will be those of his own household" (Matthew 10:34–36 NKJV).

Immediately, we can see that several symbols mentioned in the second seal are also referenced in Jesus's words. According to the second seal, the rider of the second horse takes peace from the earth and carries a sword. In Matthew 10:34, Jesus states, "Do not think that I came to bring peace on earth. I did not come to bring peace but a sword." What did Jesus mean? Did He not come to our planet in order to establish peace on earth and extend goodwill to all humanity (Luke 2:14)? Yes, this still is Jesus's ultimate goal. However, as Jesus further explained in Matthew 10:34–36 and as history bears out, the proclamation of the pure unadulterated Gospel often brings division and opposition in households, communities, and among nations.

As the first horseman proclaims the Gospel, he is followed by a second horseman, who symbolizes the opposition and persecution that the Christian church has faced. The great sword which this horseman carries is the Word of God (Matthew 10:34; Hebrews 4:12). The rider of the second horse, therefore, corresponds to the period of persecution unleashed on the church by the Roman emperors (c. AD 100–313).

By the end of the first century, almost all of the apostles had been martyred. Roman emperors, such as Nero, Domitian, and Trajan, were trying to save paganism; the result was that thousands of Christians were massacred. The Christians who would not renounce their religion were mauled by lions in Roman colosseums; others were beheaded, crucified, or burned at the stake. Hence, a "fiery red" horse is an apt symbol for this period as it represents the blood of the saints.

The final and most vicious onslaught carried out against Christians was the Diocletian persecution that lasted from AD 303 to 313. Jesus foretold this event in His letter to the Christian community in Smyrna (Revelation 2:8–11). "Do not fear any of those things which you are about to suffer. Indeed, the devil is about to throw some of you into prison, that you may be tested, and you will have tribulation ten days. Be faithful until death, and I will give you the crown of life" (Revelation 2:10 NKJV). Bible students know that a day in prophecy is often used to represent a literal year (Ezekiel 4:6). Therefore, when Jesus told the believers that they would suffer tribulation or persecution for ten days, He literally meant ten years (i.e., AD 303–313).

During the reign of Diocletian, a movement arose that was intent on reviving the old pagan religion in Rome. It is believed that Diocletian was persuaded by his adopted son and successor, Galerius, to exterminate the Christian religion from the empire. Church historian Bruce L. Shelly writes that "imperial edicts followed, commanding officials to destroy church buildings, prohibit Christian worship, and burn the scriptures. Bishops were rounded up wholesale, imprisoned, tortured, and many put to death, while the power of the imperial throne was turned loose to wipe out the rest of the Christian community in blood."[12]

THE THIRD SEAL

> When He opened the third seal, I heard the third living creature say, "Come and see." So I looked, and behold, a black horse, and he who sat on it had a pair of scales in his hand. And I heard a voice in the midst of the four living creatures saying, "A quart of wheat for a denarius, and three quarts of barley for a denarius; and do not harm the oil and the wine." (Revelation 6:5–6 NKJV)

When Jesus opens the third seal, a rider on a black horse appears. Black is the opposite of white. If the white horse represents the Gospel in its purity, truth, and righteousness, then the black horse likely symbolizes the promulgation of erroneous or false doctrines by the church. There are several important symbols in this seal. First, the horseman is seen to have a pair of scales in his hands. We are told that a quart of wheat and three quarts of barley goes for a denarius. Also, the horseman is told not to harm the oil and the wine.

Grain, oil, and wine were important food staples in ancient Palestine. A denarius was equivalent to a day's wage. After receiving his denarius, a day laborer would head to the market to buy food for his family. If a quart of wheat is carefully weighed on scales and sold to him for his entire day's wage, then he is in trouble because this will not be enough to feed his family. In all likelihood, a famine in the land has caused a scarcity of wheat and barley in the economy that would explain the price hike on these items (Ezekiel 4:16–17).

Wheat and barley are typically used to make bread. However, the message of the third seal is not concerned with literal but spiritual bread. The Bible often equates bread to the Word of God (John 6:35–58). Commenting on the third seal, Stefanovic writes, "The rejection of the gospel results in a famine of God's word, similar to the spiritual famine prophesied by Amos concerning the Israelites [Amos 8:11–13]."[13] We should also note the third horseman is told not to harm the oil and wine. What does this mean? In the Bible, oil is often used to represent the Holy Spirit, while wine represents the salvation we received through Jesus's shed blood. This means, as Paulien explains it, that "the gospel has been obscured [during this period of history] but its benefits [the Holy Spirit and salvation through Christ] are still available."[14]

At what point in history did the pure, unadulterated Gospel begin to be obscured, causing a famine for God's Word? For this, we will need to briefly examine Jesus's message to the church at Pergamos that comes immediately after His message to the church of Smyrna, the church persecuted by the Roman emperors. The word *Pergamos* means *height, elevation, or exaltation*; hence, we could say that another name for the church of Pergamos is the elevated church. Interestingly, immediately after the Diocletian persecutions, something quite remarkable happened. Christianity became the favored religion of the Roman Empire! The church was elevated! How did this happen?

In AD 312, in a bid to secure the imperial throne in Rome for himself, Constantine confronted his rival Maxentius at the Milvian Bridge that spans the Tiber River in Rome. Maxentius's army was far superior to Constantine's, yet Constantine, with unusual confidence, advanced across Milvian Bridge and defeated Maxentius. Constantine attributed his remarkable victory to the Christian God, who he said had shown him in a dream a sign of the cross in the sky with the words "In this sign, conqueror."

As an expression of his gratitude to the Christian God, Constantine issued the Edict of Milan in AD 313 that proclaimed religious toleration throughout the Roman Empire. With this edict, persecution against Christians ceased. Throughout his reign, Constantine did all he could to support the Christian religion and its leadership until, over time, Christianity became the favored religion of the empire. In AD 321, in a shrewd political move designed to unite both pagans and Christians in the empire, Constantine—himself a worshipper of the sun god Apollo—declared Sunday as a public holy day or holiday. This tradition continues today.

We are also told that "Constantine, in order to recommend the new religion [Christianity] to the heathen, transferred into it the outward ornaments to which they had been accustomed."[15] The result was that, over time, nominally converted pagans flocked into the Christian church and brought with them pagan practices, such as the use of holy water, incense, candles, lamps, processions, sacerdotal vestments, chants, images, the ring in marriage, and the practice of turning to the east.[16]

The rider of the third horse, therefore, represents the period AD 313–538 in history when the pure, unadulterated Word of God began to be obscured by a strange mixture of pagan practices. The result was a scarcity of the true Gospel. Addressing the Christians living during this period, Jesus stated that they were compromising their biblical Christian values with the pagan ideas of Rome. He told them that they were engaged in an illicit relationship that He did not agree with. He appealed to them to turn away from these ideas and practices and return to Him and the true Gospel (Revelation 2:14–16). Christians during this period paid a steep price for Roman toleration and then the elevation of the church.

The price? The compromise of their faith.

THE FOURTH SEAL

When He opened the fourth seal, I heard the voice of the fourth living creature saying, "Come and see." So I looked, and behold, a pale horse. And the name of him who sat on it was Death, and Hades followed with him. And power was given to them over a fourth of the earth, to kill with sword, with hunger, with death, and by the beasts of the earth. (Revelation 6:7–8 NKJV)

As the fourth seal is opened, John sees a hideous pale horse galloping over the horizon. As the horse strides closer, he notices that, like the pallor of a decomposing corpse, this horse is a yellowish green. Its rider is Death, the Grim Reaper himself, and in his devastating trail, he unleashes wars, famine, and disease on a quarter of the world's population.

It might be tempting to speculate, as some do, that this fourth horseman represents a future antichrist and the reign of terror that he unleashes. However, with the opening of each seal, Jesus is opening a new chapter in the prophetic history of the Christian church, which begins in John's day and ends with His Second Coming after the seventh seal is opened. Hence, the first four seals of the four horsemen of the apocalypse are heaven's prophetic description of the evolution of the Christian church in history, starting with the apostolic church and culminating with the medieval one.

The pale greenish color of the fourth horse, comparable to the shade of a corrupted or decomposing corpse, is an apt description of the medieval church. Nineteenth-century English historian John Dalberg-Acton famously stated that "power tends to corrupt, and absolute power corrupts absolutely." This is exactly what happened to the church in the Middle Ages. In His letter to the church of Thyatira, the medieval church, Jesus made clear that the church was engaging in sexual immortality. By this, He meant that the church was engaging in an ongoing illicit relationship with the state (Revelation 2:20). Comparing the medieval church to Jezebel of the Old Testament, the queen and false prophetess of ancient Israel, Jesus expressed His dissatisfaction that the church had led many believers astray with her false doctrines and that she even encouraged idolatry. He emphatically called on the medieval church to repent of her rebellion (Revelation 2:20–23).

The Roman church's compromise with the state eventually led to apostasy and the corrupting of the Gospel. By the Middle Ages, church dogma was very different from the Gospel proclaimed in apostolic times. The historian LeRoy Froom writes,

Christianity gradually became perverted into a strange mixture in which the original gospel elements changed to the point of being virtually unrecognizable in the medieval church. Repentance became penance; baptism was transformed into a regenerating rite, sprinkling being substituted for immersion. The Lord's supper was gradually changed into an atoning sacrifice, offered continually through the mass by an earthy priest, with mediatorial value claimed for both living and dead. The sign of the cross, prayers for the dead, and the veneration of martyrs, all admittedly unscriptural, developed further into the crucifix, purgatory, and saint and image worship.[17]

As Christianity became the preferred religion of the Roman Empire, Constantine and his successors granted the bishop of Rome increasingly more spiritual as well as temporal powers until, over time, the Roman church had accumulated vast wealth and power. Froom adds that "growing more and more imperial, the Roman church lost its early purity and simplicity. Her bishops grew more and more lordly and her system of government more Roman. Ecclesiastical power became the object of her eager ambition."[18]

Styling himself as the preeminent leader of all churches on earth, the Roman bishop or pope eventually emerged as the de facto ruler of Europe during medieval times. The result was that the church came to dominate all aspects of European life for over a thousand years until Napoleon took the pope prisoner in 1798.

During medieval times, the church largely withheld the Bible from the masses, and the resulting famine for the Word of God led to spiritual decline. Yet there were always pockets of faithful Christian communities throughout Europe, like the Albigenses of southern France and the Waldenses of the Alpine valleys in northern Italy, who resolved to remain true to the Word of God and their testimony of Jesus Christ. Instead of proclaiming the life-giving Gospel that enlightens the lives of men, the medieval church became tyrannical and despotic; the masses were often compelled to accept her false dogmas.

With the creation of the Inquisition, a church court created to prosecute heretics, many Bible-believing Christians, including the Albigenses and Waldenses, were imprisoned, tortured, butchered, or burned at the stake. A conservative estimate puts the number of Christians who were systematically killed during this period at about 50 million. Even as the cry for reform grew louder by the sixteenth century, the church employed every tool at its disposal to smother the Reformation. As if omens of a dark age, during this period, there were also devastating wars, famines, and pandemics.

THE FIFTH SEAL

> When He opened the fifth seal, I saw under the altar the souls of those who had been slain for the word of God and for the testimony which they held. And they cried with a loud voice, saying, "How long, O Lord, holy and true, until You judge and avenge our blood on those who dwell on the earth?" Then a white robe was given to each of them; and it was said to them that they should rest a little while longer, until both the number of their fellow servants and their brethren, who would be killed as they were, was completed. (Revelation 6:9–11 NKJV)

Throughout the book of Revelation, God's faithful people who face persecution or martyrdom are often described as those who keep the Word of God and have the testimony of faith of Jesus (Revelation 12:17; Revelation 14:12). John identifies with the persecuted saints because he himself had been exiled for "the word of God and the testimony of Jesus Christ" (Revelation 1:9). As the fifth seal opens, John sees the souls of those who have been slaughtered for "the word of God and for the testimony which they held" crying out to God under an altar for justice (Revelation 6:9).

As with the first four seals, the fifth seal uses symbolic language. John is not telling us that dead saints have somehow become undead and that they are literally crying out to God. The language is allegorical. The fifth seal of Revelation likely symbolizes an acknowledgment by heaven of the terrible atrocities committed against God's people. The fifth seal is intended to communicate God's promise that He will bring judgment and justice to His enemies who have persecuted His people. The fifth seal is opened after the fourth seal, in which the medieval church went to war against the saints of God and overcame them, committing horrendous monstrosities.

W. E. H. Lecky writes,

> That the Church of Rome has shed more innocent blood than any other institution that has ever existed among mankind, will be questioned by no Protestant who has a competent knowledge of history. The memorials, indeed, of many of her persecutions are now so scanty, that it is impossible to form a complete conception of the multitude of her victims, and it is quite certain that no power of imagination can adequately realize their sufferings.[19]

In the fifth seal, God is acknowledging to the universe and to us that He knows what His enemies have done to His people. There is a cry of how long. How long will it be before God sits in judgment against those who have persecuted His people? How long will it be before He avenges their death?

In our fallen and broken world, our human justice systems are often rooted in selfishness, bias, and unfairness. The Bible assures us though that as part of His plan to cleanse the universe of sin, the Creator God has appointed a day in history in which He will carefully examine the choices that we have all made, whether for good or evil, and reward us based on our actions. The good news is that God's adjudication is fair, impartial, and righteous. In the fifth seal, because they have accepted the salvation that Jesus offers them, God declares that these faithful martyrs are worthy of eternal life and gives them all white robes (Revelation 6:11).

The martyrs under the fifth seal are told to rest a little while longer until all Christians who would be killed are killed (Revelation 6:11). This implies that God's enemies will continue to persecute His saints until Jesus's Second Coming.

THE SIXTH SEAL

> I looked when He opened the sixth seal, and behold, there was a great earthquake; and the sun became black as sackcloth of hair, and the moon became like blood. And the stars of heaven fell to the earth, as a fig tree drops its late figs when it is shaken by a mighty wind. Then the sky receded as a scroll when it is rolled up, and every mountain and island was moved out of its place. And the kings of the earth, the great men, the rich men, the commanders, the mighty men, every slave and every free man, hid themselves in the caves and in the rocks of the mountains, and said to the mountains and rocks, "Fall on us and hide us from the face of Him who sits on the throne and from the wrath of the Lamb! For the great day of His wrath has come, and who is able to stand?" (Revelation 6:12–17 NKJV)

A series of portentous phenomena occur in the heavens and on earth with the opening of the sixth seal. There is a great earthquake. The sun becomes dark. The moon turns to blood, and the stars fall from the heavens. How should we interpret these events?

We first need to note that these occurrences are intended to be literal and not figurative. Why? Notice that John writes that the sun is as black *as* sackcloth of hair; the moon becomes *like* blood, and the stars fall *as* the late figs from a tree that is shaken. Jon Paulien notes perceptively that with this literary construction, the words *as* and *like* are being used to compare actual events to figurative analogies.[20] During the eighteenth and nineteenth centuries, a series of events transpired that several Bible scholars believe were a fulfillment of the events described here. Let us start with the great earthquake. John writes, "When He opened the sixth seal, and behold, there was a great earthquake" (Revelation 6:12 NKJV).

On All Saints' Day, November 1, 1755, while much of Lisbon's population was packed into churches for morning mass, the earth shook violently beneath their feet. Christian Staqueler, the consul of the German city of Hamburg, described it. "First we heard a rumble, like the noise of a carriage, it became louder and louder, until it was as loud as the loudest noise of a gun, immediately after that we felt the first tremble."[21] The earthquake, estimated to be about 8.4 on the Richter scale, lasted for about five minutes and has been marked as "a seminal event in European history." The convulsion was centered in the Atlantic Ocean, about 120 miles west southwest of Cape Vincente, Portugal, but its effects were far. Tremors were felt all over Europe and as far as the Caribbean. The earthquake generated one of the largest tsunamis in European history, with shock waves reaching as far as the coast of Brazil.

In Lisbon, the violent sway of the earth caused buildings to collapse, killing and injuring thousands. In the ensuing panic, thousands headed for the open public areas of the city's seaport and, upon arrival, were met with a strange sight. The sea had disappeared! Within minutes, the sea returned. It rushed into the harbor as a forty-foot-high wave at thirty miles per hour. The tsunami destroyed Lisbon's harbor and swept thousands out to sea. In the ensuing days, fires devoured what the earthquake had failed to topple. An estimated 60,000 people perished.[22]

> The sun became black as sackcloth of hair, and the
> moon became like blood. (Revelation 6:12 NKJV)

Each year at different points on the earth, the sun is obscured by the moon during a solar eclipse. These solar eclipses do not create total darkness because the sun's corona is still visible around the edges of the moon. On Friday, May 19, 1780, parts of New England and eastern Canada witnessed a strange phenomenon. By midday on that day, total darkness had engulfed the land. This was an extraordinary event because it was not caused by a solar eclipse, a volcanic eruption, or a comet collision. In the early 2000s, scientists theorized that the Dark Day and the blood moon that followed were probably caused massive forest fires in eastern Canada. They surmised that the heavy black plumes of smoke released into the air somehow grew in density because of unusually foggy atmospheric conditions. It was this dense, black soot, they said, that gradually obscured the sun.

Whatever the cause, in describing the Dark Day of 1780, Harvard Professor Samuel Williams wrote, "The fowls retired to roost, the cocks were crowing all around, as at break of day; objects could not be distinguished but at a very little distance; and everything bore the appearance of gloom of night."[23] Not able to continue their day's work, people gathered in churches and taverns. Many sought out their pastors, asked for impromptu sermons, and confessed their sins.

"A very general opinion prevailed that the day of judgment was at hand," wrote clergyman Timothy Dwight.[24] That night was especially dark, and like the blood moon of a lunar eclipse, the moon took on an unusually reddish hue.

> The stars of heaven fell to the earth, as a fig tree drops its late figs when it is shaken by a mighty wind. (Revelation 6:13 NKJV)

Every November, the Leonid meteor shower lights up the heavens in a spectacular display as meteors streak across the sky at nearly 161,000 miles per hour, which is forty-five miles a second. This happens when the earth's orbit intersects the path of Comet Tempel-Tuttle, which circles the sun once every 33.3 years. As the earth crosses the comet's path, it enters its debris field, and the result is that thousands of space rocks or meteors are unwittingly plunged into our atmosphere in a striking display as "falling stars."

Just before dawn on November 13, 1833, people all over the southeastern United States were awakened by knocks on their doors and a great commotion in the streets as awe-stricken and terrified citizens gathered to witness the usually spectacular meteor shower. During this time, a great religious revival called the Second Great Awakening was sweeping the US; many thought that the falling stars signaled judgment day. This event is still remembered in American history as "the Night the Stars Fell."[25]

By themselves, there is nothing unusual about an earthquake, burning forests that obscure the sun and moon, or falling stars caused by the Leonid meteor showers. Instead, these seminal or influential events serve as prophetic signposts in history. An important interpretative key for unlocking the significance of the phenomena that occur with the opening of the sixth seal is Matthew 24:29. In the synoptic apocalypse of Matthew 24, Jesus is asked by His disciples what would be the sign of His Second Coming and the end of the world. After describing the tribulations that His followers would have to endure throughout the centuries, Jesus tells them,

> Immediately after the tribulation of those days the sun will be darkened, and the moon will not give its light; the stars will fall from heaven, and the

powers of the heavens will be shaken. (Matthew 24:29 NKJV)

Clearly, Jesus is describing the events seen in the opening of the sixth seal. Notice that even though he does not include the great earthquake, the events are given in the same chronological order as in the sixth seal: the sun darkens, the moon is affected, and the stars fall from heaven. What is most significant here though is that Jesus states that these signs were to take place after a tribulation or persecution of His people.

We know that in the timeline or chronology of the seals, the last time God's people endured tribulation was at the hands of the medieval church during the Middle Ages, which is described in the fourth seal. By the late eighteenth century, the persecuting power of the medieval church was largely curtailed. Bible scholars heralded these seminal events: the Lisbon earthquake of 1755, the Dark Day of 1780 and falling stars of 1833, as fulfillments of the opening of the sixth seal.

These omens in heaven and earth at the opening of the sixth seal serve as chronological markers, or signposts, pointing toward the nearness of Jesus's Second Coming. Perhaps the most important takeaway from the phenomena at the opening of the sixth seal is the revelation that we are currently living under the sixth seal. In describing our present age, Luke writes, "There will be signs in the sun, in the moon, and in the stars; and on the earth distress of nations, with perplexity, the sea and the waves roaring; men's hearts failing them from fear and the expectation of those things which are coming on the earth, for the powers of the heavens will be shaken" (Luke 21:25–26 NKJV).

Undoubtedly, the last two hundred years of world history have seen astounding and rapid human progress in science, technology, and economics. The Industrial Revolution, which began in Britain in the eighteenth century, brought the rise of the machine. The result is that the agrarian way of life has largely been displaced by factories and crowded cities. Over the same two hundred years, the number of people living on the planet has exploded exponentially, with the world's population projected to reach 9.8 billion in 2050. The result has been overcrowded cities, increased industrialization, the taxing of the planet's natural resources, and the pollution of our oceans and rivers.

As two world wars tragically illustrated, the mechanization of warfare has now given us the ability to unleash mass devastation. Indeed, having discovered the secret of unleashing the power of the atom and the ability to deploy virulent biological microbes, we now have the capacity to destroy ourselves many times over. It is these sobering existential realities which Jesus foresaw in our day when He spoke of the "distress of nations, with perplexity, the sea and the waves roaring; men's hearts failing them from fear and the expectation of those things which are coming on the earth, for the powers of the heavens will be shaken" (Luke 21:25–26 NKJV).

THE HOUR OF GOD'S JUDGMENT HAS COME

> The kings of the earth, the great men, the rich men, the commanders, the mighty men, every slave and every free man, hid themselves in the caves and in the rocks of the mountains, and said to the mountains and rocks, "Fall on us and hide us from the face of Him who sits on the throne and from the wrath of the Lamb! For the great day of His wrath has come, and who is able to stand?" (Revelation 6:15–17 NKJV)

The portentous phenomena at the opening of the sixth seal also herald significant events in heaven and on earth. Bible readers have long interpreted Revelation 6:15–17 as a description of the Second Coming of Jesus. However, in the context of the seven seals, the passage is not specifically describing Jesus's Second Coming. More specifically, the text talks about the wrath of the Lamb and the great day of God's wrath and pointedly asks, "Who is able to stand?" "Who will be saved out of it?"

Why does John describe God as wrathful? Does a God of love ever get so wrathful, so angry, so vengeful that in an emotional tirade He loses His sense of reason and fairness? No. God tells us, "As surely as I live ... I take no pleasure in the death of wicked people. I only want them to turn from their wicked ways so they can live. Turn! Turn from your wickedness ... why should you die?" (Ezekiel 33:11 NLT). God is patient and longsuffering and not willing that anyone should perish (2 Peter 3:9). God's wrath then has to do with His righteous indignation, His sense of justice and fairness, and His reaction to those who rebel against Him and mistreat His people.

In order for us to gain a correct interpretation of Revelation 6:15–17, we need to examine this passage in the context of the seven seals and final chapters of Revelation that describe in detail the final events of earth's history. You will recall that under the fifth seal, there is a cry of "How long?" How long would it be before God would bring judgment and justice for the millions of faithful believers who were martyred throughout the ages? (Revelation 6:10). Also, in a parallel prophecy in the final chapters of Revelation that details the events that take place under the sixth seal, an urgent appeal is made to the people of every nation, tribe, and language to "fear God and give glory to Him, for the hour of His judgment has come" (Revelation 14:7 NKJV). Hence, when John writes that "the great day of His [God's] wrath has come, and who is able to stand?" he is telling us that under the sixth seal, the time in history has arrived when God will judge the deeds of humanity and punish the wicked.

Scripture affirms that all of humanity will have to stand before the Judgment Seat of God (2 Corinthians 5:10). He knows the thoughts and the motives of all His intelligent creatures (Hebrews 4:13). As a righteous Judge, He will always be fair and transparent.

And here is the best news of all: Jesus serves as our Judge. God the Father has turned all judgment over to Him because while on earth, Jesus walked in our shoes. He knows what it means to live in a broken, sinful world (John 5:22).

The Old Testament book of Daniel gives us a glimpse of the judgment scene in heaven convened under the sixth seal (Daniel 7:9–14). During these proceedings, the fate of all humanity is determined. In his night vision, the prophet Daniel sees a heavenly courtroom with millions of angelic witnesses ministering before God. As the Ancient of Days, God the Father takes His seat on His heavenly throne, the proceedings begin, and the books of record are opened. Even as God is all-knowing, for the benefit of all of His creatures, and in His bid to be transparent in all His dealings with His humanity, He meticulously records the lives of everyone who has lived. We know that among these books is the Lamb's book of life that contains the names of all who have ever professed faith in Jesus (Daniel 12:1; Revelation 21:27). There is also a book of remembrance in which all the deeds of humanity are transcribed (Malachi 3:16).

According to the book of Daniel, the last person to enter this heavenly tribunal is Jesus, the Son of God. Jesus enters the courtroom as a great Conqueror in the panoply of heaven's glory and takes His position before His Father as humanity's Advocate and Judge. Judgment begins first at the house of God (1 Peter 4:17), and so the life record of all who have ever pledged their lives in service to God are examined. As each name comes up in the judgment, it is Jesus, our Righteous Judge and Faithful Advocate, who makes the final determination of which names remain in the Lamb's book of life.

The judgment scene described in Daniel 7 takes place in heaven before the Second Coming because Jesus tells us, "Look, I am coming soon, bringing my reward with me to repay all people according to their deeds" (Revelation 22:12 NLT). Everyone is judged and rewarded according to their deeds. Scripture tells us that God will bring everything into judgment, whether good or evil

(Ecclesiastes 12:14). Jesus, our Righteous Judge, assures us, "All who are victorious will be clothed in white. I will never erase their names from the Book of Life, but I will announce before my Father and his angels that they are mine" (Revelation 3:5 NLT).

While the judgment continues in heaven, on earth the dragon, or Satan—knowing that His time is short—will set events in motion intended to destroy God's people. However, Jesus intervenes and will deliver His people and punish His enemies.

That's another story, the one that follows.

CHAPTER 6

TRIBULATION AND DELIVERANCE

W ill the end of the world ever happen? Commentators have long speculated that perhaps an asteroid impact, a global pandemic, solar flares, or a global war could end the world as we know it.

Yet according to the book of Revelation, the climactic event on earth, during the sixth seal, that triggers the end of the world and the Second Coming of Jesus is the great tribulation (Revelation 7:14; Revelation 13 and 14).

The prophet Daniel calls the tribulation "a time of trouble, the worst trouble the world has ever seen" (Daniel 12:1 MSG). The tribulation will be brought on by defiant and sacrilegious leaders who deceive much of the world into worshipping the beast and receiving his loathsome mark.

During the tribulation, God's faithful servants will be derided and persecuted. But God will finally intervene to punish a rebellious world in the form of seven last plagues and deliver His people. Before the tribulation escalates, a merciful God, through His faithful servants, will make one final appeal to every nation, tribe, language, and people to worship and acknowledge Him as Creator and Redeemer (Revelation 14:6–12). Many will heed God's final call and be saved.

In Revelation, John is given a glimpse into the future, where he sees an innumerable company of people from every nation, tribe, language, and people who are saved out of the tribulation, standing before the throne of God in heaven, joyfully proclaiming with a loud voice, "Salvation comes from our God who sits on the throne and from the Lamb!" (Revelation 7:9–17). Their loud, exultant acclamation to God is a direct response to the question that many had posed in the tribulation, which was this: who is able to save us (Revelation 6:17)? John in Revelation 12–14 gives us more detail of this future global crisis.

THE WOMAN, THE CHILD, AND THE DRAGON

One day, as he looks out across the Aegean Sea, John becomes transfixed by a spectacular vision of a beautiful and delicate woman with a crown of twelve stars on her head and wearing a dress as dazzling as the sun. The woman is standing on the moon and is experiencing labor pains.

Suddenly, a huge, red dragon with seven heads and ten horns stands before her, ready with its huge iron teeth to devour her baby the moment it is born. However, the woman gives birth to a son, who is later caught up to God and His throne. After giving birth, the woman escapes from the dragon into the wilderness, where she stays for 1,260 days. But the dragon goes after her. The dragon opens his mouth and vomits out a torrent of water to sweep her away. But the woman receives help from the earth that opens its mouth and swallows the floodwaters. Enraged that the woman has escaped, the dragon prepares to make war against the woman's children, those who keep God's commandments and have the testimony of Jesus.

The above narrative from Revelation 12 reads like a Hollywood script. In fact, the plotline from several Hollywood productions resembles the narrative of Revelation 12, where we find the overarching story of the Bible that describes from Genesis to Revelation the epic struggle between the forces of good and evil and humanity's need of a Savior.

The central characters in Revelation 12 are the woman, the child, and the dragon. Who do these characters portray? In scripture, God frequently uses a woman as an allegory for His people, for the nation of Israel, and later for His church (Isaiah 54:5–6; 2 Corinthians 11:2). However, even though it is the nation of Israel that brings forth the Messiah, there is a notable shift in the prophecy of Revelation 12, in which the symbol of the woman comes to preeminently symbolize Christ's true church, who as the bride of Christ shines forth resplendent in the glory of the Son of God (Revelation 12:1, 5–6; 19:7–8).

In the Bible, God's faithful people or His true church is often compared to a virtuous woman (2 Corinthians 11:2), whereas when His people rebelled into idolatry and sin, they were often likened to a lady of the night, a prostitute (Ezekiel 23; Hosea 4:15). Interestingly, both types of women, the virtuous bride and the promiscuous prostitute, appear in Revelation (Revelation 12, 17; 19:7–8).

The woman of Revelation 12 is depicted as experiencing labor pains. She represents the pregnant and expectant hope of ancient Israel that one day the Messiah or Deliverer would free them from Rome. Consequently, if the child of Revelation 12 is a symbol of Jesus the Messiah, then the dragon with seven heads and ten horns who sought to destroy Him is Rome. Herod the Great, the client king of Rome, had sought to destroy Jesus as a child, and Pontius Pilate, the Roman governor of Judaea, condemned Him as an adult to be crucified. After His crucifixion, Jesus rose from the dead and ascended triumphantly to God and to His throne (Revelation 12:5).

Another central figure in the narrative of Revelation 12 is the dragon. More than a third of Revelation 12 is dedicated to unmasking this character, Satan, the avowed enemy of God's people in Revelation (Revelation 12:9). It was Satan who was the real power behind the puppet regime of imperial Rome that tried to destroy the babe of Bethlehem. And it was by Satan's instigation that a rabid mob stood before Pilate and shouted incessantly, "Crucify him!" His malevolent work is not done yet, either.

Revelation 12 teaches that the devil's cosmic war against God and His people began in heaven and that one-third of the angels there sided with him. At the cross, the devil's true character was exposed before the universe. He was unmasked as a demented peddler of lies and a murderer (John 8:44; Revelation 12:10–11). Now confined to this planet and with his time running out, the devil launched a violent and sustained attack against the woman, God's faithful people, after Jesus ascended to heaven beyond his reach. In order to escape the wrath of the dragon, faithful Christians fled into the wilderness during the Middle Ages, into obscurity for 1,260 prophetic days, or 1,260 literal years.

After Jesus ascended to heaven, the dragon or devil employed imperial Rome, and later a corrupted medieval church, to try to destroy Jesus's followers. For over a thousand years, faithful Christians escaped into the wilderness, into the uninhabited mountain retreats of Europe, where God preserved His truth and His people. Yet the dragon, determined to annihilate them, unleashed a flood of persecution. The flood that the serpent spews from its mouth also represents a flood of false teachings that the serpent hoped would dilute and destroy God's truth. Yet even with this torrent of falsehoods, God's truth, as inscribed in His Holy Word, and His people survived (Isaiah 59:19; Revelation 12:12–15).

Revelation 12 says that the woman received help from the earth that figuratively opened its mouth and swallowed up the flood. This help for Christians came with the dawn of the Protestant Reformation and the discovery of the New World by Christopher Columbus. Many Christians emigrated to the New World in order to escape the dragon's persecution in Europe. Thus, over time, free America emerged as a place of refuge, a stronghold for persecuted peoples (Revelation 12:16).

At the conclusion of Revelation 12, the devil is infuriated that the woman has escaped. Knowing that his time is almost ended, with seething rage, he prepares a final war that he plans to unleash on the children of the woman—those who keep God's commandments and have the testimony, or faith, of Jesus (Revelation 12:17).

THE SEA BEAST

In John's day, people feared the sea and often viewed it as a place of chaos and evil, where dangerous and wild sea monsters dwelled (Psalm 74:12–14). In this context, John sees a monster with seven heads and ten horns rising from the sea. The mammoth sea creature emerges; each of its heads has a blasphemous name; one of its heads receives a deadly wound that later heals. As this sea beast surfaces, the dragon gives this monster its power, its throne, and great authority. The sea beast is permitted to continue for three and a half prophetic years and is charged with annihilating God's people. John writes that almost the entire world, those who do not have their names written in the Lamb's book of life, will be astounded and entranced at the reappearance of the sea beast and pledge their allegiance to him after he receives a deadly wound but comes back to life.

Who does this hideous sea beast represent? Today many believe that the sea beast is symbolic of a future antichrist who will arise somewhere in Europe to eventually wreak havoc on the world. According to this scenario, this future antichrist will resemble Nicolae Carpathia, the fictional character created by Tim LaHaye and Jerry B. Jenkins in their popular Left Behind book series. In Left Behind, like the fictional bloodsucking Dracula, the antichrist, Nicolae Carpathia, hails from Transylvania, Romania, and eventually grows in power and highjacks the leadership of the United Nations. After three and a half years, Carpathia is assassinated but miraculously rises from the dead to the amazement of the entire world. Declaring that he is god, Carpathia begins a reign of terror when he enters a rebuilt temple in Jerusalem, desecrates it, and declares that all peoples and nations worship him and the image of himself that he sets up in the Jewish temple. He eventually plunges the planet into a worldwide Armageddon but is defeated at the return of Jesus.

Good reasons exist, however, not to believe this above scenario.

First, according to the apocalyptic book of Daniel, a beast in biblical prophecy is typically used to represent a nation or world power, not an individual (Daniel 7:23). It is true that these beast powers will usually have a man like a king, president, or caesar at their head. However, in apocalyptic prophecy, the dominant idea is that a beast symbolizes a political power or kingdom.

Second, we have often believed that the sea beast will be an antichristian power that arises to oppose God's people in the last days. But is this true? The apostle Paul in 2 Thessalonians 2, when commenting on the actions of the sea beast power whom he calls the lawless one, writes that the sea beast arises in the Christian church after an apostasy, a falling away, or abandonment by some Christians of certain key tenets of their faith (2 Thessalonians 2:3–4).

In his farewell address to the Ephesian church, the apostle Paul warned, "I know that as soon as I'm gone, vicious wolves are going to show up and rip into this flock, men from your very own ranks twisting words so as to seduce disciples into following them instead of Jesus. So stay awake and keep up your guard" (Acts 20:29–31 MSG). Hence, for Paul and John, the sea beast is not an antichristian power; rather, the sea beast power arises out of the Christian church itself after an abandonment of certain key principles of the Gospel.

For Revelation 13 and the apostle Paul, the travesty of the last days is a terrible deception, a strong delusion that dupes multitudes—even some Christians—into believing lies. In fact, Paul warns that believers who do not have a love for the truth as revealed in God's Word will be prime candidates for the sea beast's fatal deceptions (2 Thessalonians 2:9–12). In Matthew 24, Jesus warns that the actions of the sea beast, or false christ, will be so deceptively Christlike that, if possible, even His followers would be deceived by it (Matthew 24:24–25).

This leads us to our third point. A counterfeit is defined as something that resembles the real thing. In Revelation 13, the sea beast is designed by the dragon to shamelessly counterfeit Jesus's ministry.

The Gospels reveal that Jesus resembles His Father and that He received His throne and authority from Him. In Revelation 13, the sea beast, with seven heads and ten horns, resembles the dragon (who is himself a counterfeit of God the Father) and receives his power, throne, and great authority from Satan.

Jesus's public ministry lasted for about three and a half years; the sea beast's power continues for forty-two months, or three and a half prophetic years.

At the end of His ministry, Christ was wounded for our transgressions and later rose from the dead. Similarly, the sea beast power receives a deadly wound that later heals. In Greek, the prefix *anti,* as in *antichrist,* can also be translated as "instead of" or "in the place of." So clearly the dragon raises up the sea beast so that he can take the place of Jesus in the eyes of the masses.

So if not an antichristian power like Nicolae Carpathia, who might the sea beast be? For the people alive during the last days, during the tribulation, the sea beast will represent some kind of moral authority because the masses will heed his injunctions and worship him. The sea beast will be a Jesus wannabe, a religious as well as political world power professing Christianity. In fact, many Bible scholars believe the prophetic descriptions of the sea beast fittingly describe the activities of the Roman papacy in history and a future revival of its power.

THE BEAST FROM THE EARTH

In Revelation 13, there are two beasts. One rises out of the sea; the other out of the earth. If the sea in Revelation symbolizes a highly populated area on the planet (Revelation 17:15), then the earth would represent a sparsely populated area on the globe (Revelation 12:15–16). You will recall that at the end of Revelation 12, after the woman escapes his clutches, an enraged dragon decides to wage war on her offspring, the final generation of faithful Christians, who are described as those who keep God's commandments and have the testimony of Jesus (Revelation 12:17). Hence, it is important for us to keep in mind that the great tribulation is primarily agitated by the dragon, and he intends that it will be his final solution for Christians who remain loyal to Jesus.

In Revelation 12, the earth opens its mouth and swallows up a great flood of water that the dragon spews out at the woman. The earth opening its mouth symbolized in prophecy the opening up of new opportunities in a relatively sparsely populated New World for persecuted peoples to resettle and worship freely. But perhaps what is most disturbing is that Revelation 13 predicts that in the future, the dragon will find a way to breach the fortifications of free America and plunge the entire world into crisis.

According to Revelation 13, a beast with two horns like a lamb but that eventually speaks like a dragon will arise from the earth. Through the signs and miracles and then later through an enforced international mandate, the earth beast will cause much of the world to worship the resurrected sea beast and receive its deadly mark.

This earth beast that speaks like a dragon will accomplish its goals by creating an entity called "the image of the beast"—a religiopolitical body that will exercise all the authoritarian power that the sea beast had exerted during the dark ages. As a sign of their loyalty and allegiance to this entity, no one on the planet will be permitted to buy or sell unless they receive the mark of the sea beast on their right hand or on their forehead. By agreeing to receive the devil's mark, many will pledge their allegiance to the dragon and not to the Lamb. Over time, dissidents who refuse to worship this satanic system eventually receive the death penalty.

Like the beast that rises from the sea, the earth beast is a global world power. It is described as having two horns like a lamb. Even as the ravenous sea beast before it has ten horns, the earth beast has only two horns like a lamb. This lamblike beast that arises from the earth will be a world power that will have Christlike attributes and will be friendly to Christians—at least at first. Likely, the lamblike beast that rises from the earth represents free America. This would explain why the offspring of woman in Revelation 12 finds a refuge from the dragon's persecution in the area on the earth, from which this lamblike beast arises. However, the prophecy reveals that the character of the lamblike beast later changes as it eventually speaks as a dragon!

In order for global citizens to participate in the global economy, they will be required by the image of the beast authority to receive the dreaded mark of the beast on their right hand or on their forehead. In popular culture, the mark of the beast has come to mean many things. For some, it is the devil's number 666 that will be tattooed on the right hand or forehead; others think it will be a special computer chip implanted under the skin that enables global citizens to buy or sell. During the COVID-19 pandemic, some online conspiracy theorists and antivaxxers falsely propagated the idea that the vaccines contained elements of the mark of the beast.

So what is the truth about the mysterious mark of the beast? For us to have a correct understanding of what the mark of the beast is, we will first need to examine the idea of "worship" in Revelation.

WORSHIP HIM WHO MADE HEAVEN AND EARTH

The great tribulation scenario described in Revelation 13 reflects the story of the three Hebrew exiles, Shadrach, Meshach, and Abednego, who were thrown into a furnace for their refusal to worship King Nebuchadnezzar's golden idol. In Daniel 3, King Nebuchadnezzar sets up a golden idol in Babylon and, at its dedication, commands all Babylonian officials present to bow down and worship the idol.

Shadrach, Meshach, and Abednego courageously tell King Nebuchadnezzar that they could not comply with his order. They assured the pagan monarch that their God was more than able to deliver them from the fiery furnace, but if He chose not to, they were prepared to die rather than worship the king's idol. Enraged, the king threw the three men into the furnace. However, God miraculously intervened and protected the three men from the flames so that when they emerged, not even their clothes smelled of smoke!

As the story of the three Hebrew boys in Daniel 3 and Revelation 13 outlines, the central issue during the great tribulation that will polarize the world into two camps is worship. The dividing question will be this: *whom will you worship?*

Will you worship the Creator God and receive His seal? Or will you worship the beast and receive his mark?

Like the three faithful Hebrew boys who refused to bow down to Nebuchadnezzar's idol, those who will not worship the global satanic system will be ridiculed, persecuted, and even killed (Revelation 6:10–11; 14:12–13).

Everyone worships something, even the nonreligious. What do you cherish the most in life? What do you absolutely adore and live for? To what are you wholly devoted? What has your highest allegiance and loyalty? Many people idolize their spouse, children, career, money, sports heroes, or celebrities. An expert in Jewish law once asked Jesus what He thought the most important commandment in scripture was. Jesus answered,

> "You must love the LORD your God with all your heart, all your soul, and all your mind." This is the first and greatest commandment. A second is equally important: "Love your neighbor as yourself." The entire law and all the demands of the prophets are based on these two commandments. (Matthew 22:34–40 NLT)

Love and devotion to God is the first and greatest commandment. To worship God means that we love Him, we revere Him, and we honor Him as our Creator and Redeemer above everything else. To truly worship God means that we are wholly devoted to Him, that we adore Him, and that He holds the first place in our lives. Jesus reiterates that even as love for our fellow men is equally important, it should be secondary to our love, adoration, and devotion to God.

In His response to the Jewish lawyer in Matthew 22, Jesus was actually summarizing the Ten Commandments or Decalogue (Exodus 20:1–17). One of John's key identifying characteristics of God's faithful people in the last days is that they not only have the faith or testimony of Jesus but that they also will keep God's commandments. Faithfulness to God's commandments is one of the important themes of Revelation (Revelation 9:20–21; 12:17; 14:12; 21:7–8).

During the tribulation, the dragon will be especially incensed with believers who have faith in Jesus and who also keep God's commandments. Why would the dragon be so infuriated with these commandment-keeping Christians? When we quickly parse through the first four of the Ten Commandments, we begin to realize why. As Jesus told the Jewish lawyer, the first four commandments tell us *why* our Creator God deserves our love and worship. The first commandment tells us that God should be our only God. The second tells us that we should not have idols in our lives. The third commandment tells us not to misuse God's name, while the fourth instructs us to honor God's Sabbath day because He is the one who made us (Exodus 20:1–11; Psalm 100).

No wonder the dragon would be so angry with believers who hold to these commandment principles. It is because these commandments strike at the very heart of the dragon's obsessive ambition to be like God and his compulsive desire for worship. Indeed, as you will recall, the prophet Isaiah exposed the dragon's fanatical sacrilegious aspirations that will drive his desperate murderous activities during the tribulation.

How you are fallen from heaven, O Lucifer, son of
the morning! How you are cut down to the ground,
you who weakened the nations! For you have said
in your heart; I will ascend into heaven, I will exalt
my throne above the stars of God; I will also sit
on the mount of the congregation on the farthest
sides of the north; I will ascend above the heights
of the clouds, I will be like the Most High. (Isaiah
14:12–14 NKJV)

It's simple. The dragon wants to be like the Most High God.
And to the very end, He will crave the worship and adulation due
only to the Creator God. This is why during the tribulation, he will
set up a counterfeit trinity with himself, the sea beast, and lamblike
beast who speaks as a dragon for people to worship. By receiving
the mark of the beast and worshiping this counterfeit trinity, the
masses will be inadvertently worshipping, or paying homage, to the
devil himself.

THE MARK OF THE BEAST
OR THE SEAL OF GOD?

When the dust from the great tribulation settles, only two classes
will exist: those who worship the beast and receive his mark and
those who worship the Creator God and have His seal in their
forehead.

How then are believers sealed during the tribulation?

Scripture tells us that believers are sealed by the Holy Spirit
(2 Corinthians 1:22; Ephesians 4:30), another way of saying that
the Holy Spirit convicts us of God's truth and confirms our faith
in Jesus. Hence, during the tribulation, those who receive the seal
of God are sealed in their mind that their Creator God is worthy
of worship because He made them and has redeemed them by the
blood of the Lamb. Their sealing signifies that, like Shadrach,

Meshach, and Abednego, they have determined that nothing, not even death, will pry them from their Creator. They will follow Jesus wherever He leads.

Those who receive the seal of God will have their heavenly Father's name written on their foreheads; those who worship the sea beast will receive his mark on their forehead or on their right hand (Revelation 13:16; 14:1). John's references in Revelation 13 to being sealed in the forehead or receiving a mark on the right hand is an allusion to Deuteronomy 6 in which Moses instructs the Israelites to "tie them [God's laws] as symbols on your hands and bind them on your foreheads" (Deuteronomy 6:8 NIV).

Revelation expert Ranko Stefanovic states that some Israelites took Moses's injunction literally by wearing phylacteries, small leather boxes tied on their forehead containing texts from the law of Moses that were worn during prayer sessions.[1] However, as Stefanovic explains, when God's people receive the seal of God on their forehead, it "has to do with impressing God's law upon the minds and the behavior of His people."[2] Behind our forehead is the frontal lobe, the brain's largest lobe, which is responsible for judgment and reasoning.

Our awareness, consciousness, impressions, and convictions about God are formed in our frontal lobe. This is why John writes that God's people are sealed in their forehead. They have forever settled in their minds the truth about their Creator God and have pledged total allegiance to Jesus the Lamb. Conversely, those who receive the mark of the beast on their forehead and on their right hand are deceived by the dragon. In the end, the global push for all to receive the mark of the beast will be an attempt by the dragon to replace the imperatives or commandments of the Creator God with human systems, laws, and traditions (Daniel 7:25). During confrontations with the religious leaders, Jesus warned that their worship was futile if they dispensed with the commandments of God and embraced the traditions of men instead (Matthew 15:3–9).

To avoid receiving the mark of the beast during the tribulation, you need to faithfully keep all God's commandments, and the only way to do that is by exercising saving faith in Jesus. Then you will be secure in God and will receive His end-time seal.

THE SEVENTH SEAL

> When He opened the seventh seal, there was silence in heaven for about half an hour. And I saw the seven angels who stand before God, and to them were given seven trumpets. Then another angel, having a golden censer, came and stood at the altar. He was given much incense, that he should offer it with the prayers of all the saints upon the golden altar which was before the throne. And the smoke of the incense, with the prayers of the saints, ascended before God from the angel's hand, filled it with fire from the altar, and threw it to the earth. And there were noises, thunderings, lightnings, and an earthquake. So the seven angels who had the seven trumpets prepared themselves to sound. (Revelation 8:1–5 NKJV)

The tribulation begins under the sixth seal and concludes under the seventh. The events under the seventh seal are chronicled in Revelation 8–11, and they culminate with the announcement in heaven that the time has arrived in history for God to set up His eternal kingdom (Revelation 11:15–19). God also describes the very same events in Revelation 15:5–8 and continuing in chapter 16, though using different symbols. This would mean that the seven trumpets and the seven plagues described in Revelation are one and the same.

When Jesus opens the seventh seal, John in vision is again directed to heaven, where he observes a flurry of activity in the heavenly temple. There he sees an angelic priest who has the responsibility of offering up incense to God at a golden altar mixed with the prayers of the saints. The action of this angelic priest is reminiscent of the daily intercessory work that the priests of ancient Israel performed on behalf of the people (Exodus 30:7–8). Here again we are reminded that God hears the prayers and cries of His people when they ascend to heaven.

But there is a marked change in the activity of the angelic priest. After offering up incense with the prayers of the saints, the priest fills the censer with fire from the golden altar and then throws it into the earth. What follows are noises, thunder, lightning, and an earthquake. The implication here is that when the seventh seal is opened, heaven ceases its intercessory work for sinful humanity forever, since the censer that is used in the work of intercession is thrown away. This makes sense since the great tribulation agitates a final separation among the inhabitants of the earth in which the fate of all is forever sealed (Revelation 22:11).

Next John sees in heaven seven angels dressed in flowing white priestly robes, each having a trumpet in his hand (Revelation 8:1–2). These seven angels with the seven trumpets are reminiscent of the seven priests of Israel who blew their trumpets when God brought judgment to the heathen city of Jericho (Joshua 6:4). Later, when John is again shown the very same scene in Revelation, instead of having seven trumpets, the seven angels have seven golden bowls that contain the seven last plagues. These seven last plagues are God's judgments that He has reserved for Babylon and those with the mark of the beast (Revelation 15:6–8).

BABYLON

Babylon is introduced in Revelation 14 as the entity responsible for much of the world receiving the mark of the beast (Revelation 14:8). Babylon in Revelation is not the ancient empire of King

Nebuchadnezzar of course but a code word or symbol that represents a fallen church system that mixes the holy things of God with pagan practices (Daniel 5:1–4; Revelation 17:4). During the great tribulation, Satan will work through Babylon to deceive almost the entire (Revelation 18:1–2).

Remember there are two women in Revelation. In chapter 12, God's faithful people is represented by a woman clothed with the glory of the sun and having a crown of twelve stars on her head. In Revelation 17, John sees another woman whom God calls Babylon, an unfaithful one gorgeously dressed in purple and scarlet who is called a great prostitute. Babylon is also described as wearing beautiful "jewelry made of gold and precious gems and pearls. In her hand she held a gold goblet full of obscenities and the impurities of her immorality" (Revelation 17:4 NLT).

In Revelation 17, John sees Babylon riding the sea beast that was described in Revelation 13 (or scarlet beast as he is called in Revelation 17). If God's faithful bride in Revelation is intimately connected with Christ the Lamb and ultimately marries Him, then in contrast, Babylon is riding the sea beast because, as a fallen church, she is in a close, illicit relationship with this blasphemous entity. Not only that, but as a notorious prostitute, Babylon has illicit relationships with the nations on earth as well (Revelation 17:1–2). John describes Babylon as being drunk with the blood of the saints, meaning Babylon has killed other Christians.

God is angered by Babylon, so much so that He pours out seven devastating plagues on her and all those who join her in rebellion. Why? Because of her worldwide influence and professed association with Christ, Babylon will deceive much of the world during the tribulation into thinking that by taking the mark of the beast, they are following Jesus when, in fact, they are not! Babylon also has the blood of Christ's saints on her hands. A merciful God gave her time for repentance and reformation, but out of pride, arrogance, and satanic delusion, she refused His offers of grace and salvation (Revelation 2:20–23; 18:6–7).

Before He pours out the seven last plagues on Babylon and her adherents, God sends a final urgent message of warning to everyone in the entire world not to accept her false teachings because by doing so, they will receive the mark of the beast (Revelation 14:8). God also has His people in Babylon, and He implores them to come out of her. "I heard another voice from heaven saying, 'Come out of her, my people, lest you share in her sins, and lest you receive of her plagues. For her sins have reached to heaven, and God has remembered her iniquities'" (Revelation 18:4–5 NKJV).

As the seven last plagues fall on a rebellious planet and the world is plunged into deep darkness and chaos, global support for Babylon eventually dries up when the nations realize that they have been deceived (Revelation 16:10–12). The kings of the earth turn their wrath against Babylon and destroy her with fire (Revelation 17:15–16). Next, inspired by the dragon and his demons, the kings and the inhabitants of the earth consolidate all their forces for a particular day and hour for the battle of Armageddon on which they plan to annihilate God's people. It is here, at the darkest hour, that Jesus delivers His people (Revelation 16:13–15).

For much of the world, the Second Coming of Jesus will be a cataclysmic event; it will be an overwhelming surprise. Every eye will see Jesus. From the eastern to the western end of heaven, the sky will be lit up with millions of angels. At the center of this glorious entourage is Jesus, the King of kings and Lord of lords. The earth sways violently as the Son of God approaches. His words are a consuming fire that instantly destroys the beast, the kings (political leaders) of the earth, and all the armies arrayed against Him and His people.

As Jesus descends from heaven with the thunderous shout of a divine Conqueror, His voice literally wakes the dead. He calls forth a great company of His sleeping saints from their graves, who meet Him in the air. This is the first resurrection (John 5:28–30; Revelation 20:4–6). The saints alive at His Second Coming are also caught up to meet Jesus and the resurrected believers in the air, after which they all ascend to the Father's house, to heaven, to forever be with the Lord (1 Thessalonians 4:16–17; John 14:1–3).

THE WORLD TOMORROW

Many people are often surprised to discover that one day heaven will be on earth after our planet is restored to its Edenic beauty. Even though sin has interrupted His plans, it has always been God's will that humans would inhabit the earth. Jesus's prayer was "Your kingdom come. Your will be done on earth as it is in heaven" (Matthew 6:10 NKJV). God will one day establish His glorious eternal kingdom on earth (Daniel 2:35, 44). The redeemed of God will one day inherit the earth (Psalm 37:9; Daniel 7:27; Matthew 5:5).

At the Second Coming, Jesus will take His faithful people to heaven with Him, and they will reign with Him there for one thousand years (Revelation 20:4). After a thousand years, Jesus and His saints return to earth with the city of God, the New Jerusalem. It is also at this time that the second resurrection takes place, the resurrection of everyone who has ever lived on the earth but whose names are not written in the Lamb's book of life (Revelation 20:5, 6–15). During the thousand years, Satan and his fallen angels are confined to a desolate earth devoid of human life (Revelation 20:1–3). After the dead come back to life at the second resurrection, Satan deceives them all into believing that if they raise a mighty army, they can storm the New Jerusalem and take it for themselves.

Revelation tells us that Satan will mobilize an army as immense "as the sand of the sea" that will surround the city of God (Revelation 20:7–9). But a fire, a great conflagration prepared by God for Satan and his angels, will come out of heaven and destroy the dragon, his angels, and all those who side with them. Those destroyed will never live again (Isaiah 47:14; Ezekiel 28:18–19; Psalm 37:10, 20; Matthew 25:41). This devouring inferno that John describes in Revelation as a lake of fire will purge the earth of every trace of sin and evil (2

Peter 3:10). Sin and sinners will never again arise on the earth or in God's universe (Nahum 1:9). There will be nothing left but ashes (Malachi 4:1–3).

After the curse of sin is removed from the earth by fire, God will restore the earth to its former Edenic beauty (Revelation 21:1). God says, "Behold, I make all things new" (Revelation 21:5 NKJV). The world of tomorrow will be as real as our world today, only better. Today about 70 percent of our planet is covered with water; however, in the new earth, John did not see any briny oceans or seas (Revelation 21:1). Our planet will be a vast unending paradise filled with majestic mountains, rolling hills, evergreen forests, and lush, colorful gardens with flowers of every variety (Isaiah 35:1–2). Regarding the animal life, the prophet Isaiah writes,

> In that day the wolf and the lamb will live together; the leopard will lie down with the baby goat. The calf and the yearling will be safe with the lion, and a little child will lead them all. The cow will graze near the bear. The cub and the calf will lie down together. The lion will eat hay like a cow. The baby will play safely near the hole of a cobra. Yes, a little child will put its hand in a nest of deadly snakes without harm. Nothing will hurt or destroy in all my holy mountain, for as the waters fill the sea, so the earth will be filled with people who know the LORD. (Isaiah 11:6–9 NLT)

There will be no crime, sickness, death, or crying; all these things have passed away (Isaiah 35:5–6; Isaiah 60:18; Revelation 21:4). Even as they will be blessed with glorified bodies and eternal youth, the redeemed will recognize each other (1 Corinthians 13:12). In the happiness, joy, and bliss of the new earth, people will run and never get tired. They will walk and not faint. They will even mount up with wings like eagles (Isaiah 40:31). There will be many exciting new treasures to explore in the new earth and in God's universe. People will build houses and inhabit them; they will plant vineyards and enjoy their fruit (Isaiah 65:21–22).

But for me, perhaps the most exciting and thrilling thing about the new earth is that God Himself will be there, and I will see His face (Revelation 22:4)! God will move the headquarters of the universe to the new earth! When John sees the New Jerusalem, the city of God, coming down from heaven to the earth, he hears a loud voice in heaven proclaiming, "Behold, the tabernacle of God is with men, and He will dwell with them, and they shall be His people. God Himself will be with them and be their God" (Revelation 21:3 NKJV).

The home of God on earth will be a spectacular and breathtaking place where the redeemed will gather weekly and monthly (Isaiah 66:22–23). It will be the capital of the new earth. Based on the descriptions and measurements provided in Revelation, we know that the New Jerusalem will be a magnificent city, a perfect cube, with length, width, and height of about 1,400 miles (Revelation 21:9–21). This means that the height of the city will extend way beyond our atmosphere. To put this another way, someone said that "if you are one mile away from the city, you would not see the top, but if you are ten miles away, you just might. At 5,000 miles away, it would appear more than 130 times larger than the moon. To appear the size of the moon, you would have to be 160,427 miles away."[3]

If everyone who has ever lived were saved in the end, there would be plenty of room in the New Jerusalem! John tells us that the throne of God and of the Lamb will be inside the city. A river of life, clear as crystal, will flow from the throne of God; the tree of life will be in the center of the New Jerusalem (Revelation 22:1–2). There will be no night in the city because the glory of God and of the Lamb will fill this celestial tabernacle (Revelation 21:23–24; 22:5).

We can be hopeful about tomorrow because God has given

us wonderful glimpses of the amazing future that He has planned for us! Jesus came to our broken world in order to lead us into that glorious future. He is the beginning and the end, the alpha and omega of our hopes and dreams, the man who holds tomorrow.

NOTES

Chapter 1

1   https://9-11commission.gov/report/911Report_Exec.pdf (July 2004), 1.

2   https://9-11commission.gov/report/911Report_Exec.pdf (July 2004), 1.

3   https://9-11commission.gov/report/911Report_Exec.pdf (July 2004), 1, 2.

4   https://9-11commission.gov/report/911Report_Exec.pdf (July 2004), 6.

5   Emily Eakin, "Suddenly, It's Nostradamus, the Best Seller," *New York Times* (September 18, 2001).

6   Emily Eakin, "Suddenly, It's Nostradamus, the Best Seller."

7   Stephan Schwartz, "An Arrow through Time," November 12, 2010, https://stephanschwartz.com/an-arrow-through-time.

8   Tom Chivers, "'Web-Bot Project' Makes Prophecy of 2012 Apocalypse" (Telegraph Media Group, September 24, 2009), https://www.telegraph.co.uk/technology/news/6227357/Web-bot-project-makes-prophecy-of-2012-apocalypse.html.

9   Stephan Schwartz, "Crisis Conduct Program by Stephan A. Schwartz" (Nemoseen Media, May 8, 2020), https://www.nemoseen.com/crisis-conduct.

10 Quentin Hardy, "The Future Is Not What It Used to Be" *(Forbes* magazine, July 19, 2012), https://www.forbes.com/2007/10/13/pessimism-paramaibo-tech-future07-cz_qh_1015hardy.html?sh=4218cb907d04.

11 Leo Tolstoy, *Confessions—Arvindguptatoys,* translated by David Patterson (New York: WW Norton & Company, 1983). Accessed November 21, 2021, https://arvindguptatoys.com/arvindgupta/confessions-tolstoy.pdf.

12 James Randi, *The Mask of Nostradamus: The Prophecies of the World's Most Famous Seer* (Amherst, NY: Prometheus Books, 1998), 140.

13 Edgar Leoni, *Nostradamus and His Prophecies* (Mineola, NY: Dover Publications, 2000), 110.

14 Edgar Leoni, *Nostradamus and His Prophecies*, 9.

15 Edgar Leoni, *Nostradamus and His Prophecies*, 127.

16 James Randi, *The Mask of Nostradamus: The Prophecies of the World's Most Famous Seer*, 36.

17 Edgar Leoni, *Nostradamus and His Prophecies*, 110.

18 "Nostradamus Prediction about 9/11." Accessed November 21, 2021, https://stcaf.blogspot.com/2012/11/nostradamus-pridiction.html.

19 Edgar Leoni, *Nostradamus and His Prophecies*, 327.

20 Edgar Leoni, *Nostradamus and His Prophecies*, 26.

21 Rene Noorbergen, *Ellen G. White, Prophet of Destiny* (Brushton, NY: TEACH Services, 2001), 17.

22 Rene Noorbergen, *Ellen G. White, Prophet of Destiny,* 17.

23 LeRoy Froom, *The Prophetic Faith of Our Fathers*, vol. 1 (Hagerstown, MD: Review and Herald, 1978), 28.

24 Sir Isaac Newton Quotes, S. Austin Allibone, comp., *1880 Prose Quotations from Socrates to Macaulay.* Accessed January 21, 2022, https://www.bartleby.com/349/authors/149.html.

25 Lee Strobel, *The Case for Faith: A Journalist Investigates the Toughest Objections to Christianity* (Grand Rapids, MI, Zondervan, 2004), 131–133.

Chapter 2

1 William H. Shea, *Daniel: A Reader's Guide* (Nampa, ID: Pacific Press Pub. Association, 2005), 34.

2 William Whiston and Paul L. Maier, *The New Complete Works of Josephu*s (Grand Rapids, MI: Kregel Publications, 1999), 356.

3 R. B. Strassler, *The Landmark Herodotus: The Histories* (NY: Anchor Books, 2009), 96, 97.

4 R. B. Strassler, *The Landmark Herodotus: The Histories*, 97.

5 William H. Shea, *Daniel: A Reader's Guide*, 40.

6 William H. Shea, *Daniel: A Reader's Guide*, 40.

7 "Dreaming" *(Psychology Today* [n.d.]. Accessed November 21, 2021, https://www.psychologytoday.com/us/basics/dreaming.

8 J. B. Doukhan, *Secrets of Daniel: Wisdom and Dreams of a Jewish Prince in Exile* (Hagerstown, MD: Review and Herald Publishing Association, 2000), 24.

9 William H. Shea, *Daniel: A Reader's Guide*, 96.

10 J. B. Doukhan, *Secrets of Daniel: Wisdom and Dreams of a Jewish Prince in Exile*, 26.

11 LeRoy Froom, *The Prophetic Faith of Our Fathers*, vol. 1 (Hagerstown, MD: Review and Herald Publishing Association, 1978), 40.

12 William H. Shea, *Daniel: A Reader's Guide,* 100.

13 J. B. Doukhan, *Secrets of Daniel: Wisdom and Dreams of a Jewish Prince in Exile,* 29.

14 William H. Shea, *Daniel: A Reader's Guide*, 58.

15 William H. Shea, *Daniel: A Reader's Guide*, 58.

16 R. B. Strassler, *The Landmark Herodotus: The Histories*, 102.

17 R. B. Strassler, *The Landmark Herodotus: The Histories*, 102.

18 R. B. Strassler, *The Landmark Herodotus: The Histories*, 102.

19 R. B. Strassler, *The Landmark Herodotus: The Histories*, 102.

20 J. B. Doukhan, *Secrets of Daniel: Wisdom and Dreams of a Jewish Prince in Exile*, 32.

21 J. B. Doukhan, *Secrets of Daniel: Wisdom and Dreams of a Jewish Prince in Exile*, 31.

22 Edward Gibbon, *The History of the Decline and Fall of the Roman Empire*, vol. 2, 1776, 442.

23 J. B. Doukhan, *Secrets of Daniel: Wisdom and Dreams of a Jewish Prince in Exile*, 33.

24 J. B. Doukhan, *Secrets of Daniel: Wisdom and Dreams of a Jewish Prince in Exile*, 33.

25 J. B. Doukhan, *Secrets of Daniel: Wisdom and Dreams of a Jewish Prince in Exile*, 34.

26 J. B. Doukhan, *Secrets of Daniel: Wisdom and Dreams of a Jewish Prince in Exile*, 37.

27 J. B. Doukhan, *Secrets of Daniel: Wisdom and Dreams of a Jewish Prince in Exile*, 41.

Chapter 3

1 Lee Strobel, *The Case for Christ* (Michigan: Zondervan Publishing House, 1998), 141.

2 William H. Shea, *Daniel: A Reader's Guide* (Idaho: Pacific Press Publishing Association, 2005), 20.

3 David Alexander, Pat Alexander, *Zondervan Handbook to the Bible* (Michigan: Zondervan Publishing House, 2002), 94.

4 Jason Lisle, *Taking Back Astronomy* (Arizona: Master Books, 2006), 14.

5 Jason Lisle, *Taking Back Astronomy*, 23.

6 Timothy Keller, *The Reason for God: Belief in an Age of Skepticism* (London, England: Penguin Books, 2008), 227.

7 Lee Strobel, *The Case for Faith: A Journalist Investigates the Toughest Objections to Christianity* (Michigan: Zondervan Publishing House, 2004), 27.

8   Morris L. Venden, *To Know God: A 5-Day Plan* (Maryland: Review and Herald Publishing Association, 2010), 22.

Chapter 4

1   Dwight K. Nelson, *What 'Left Behind' Left Behind* (Review and Herald Pub. Association: 2001), 41.
2   https://wheatonbillygraham.com/wp-content/uploads/2021/09/Rural-Theology.doc.
3   Lee Strobel, *The Case for Christ* (Grand Rapids, MI, Zondervan, 1998), 235.
4   Billy Graham Evangelistic Association (n.d.), "Following Jesus Is Not a Burden!" Accessed November 21, 2021, https://billygraham.org/answer/following-jesus-is-not-a-burden/.

Chapter 5

1   A. M. Rodriguez, *Future Glory: The 8 Greatest End-time Prophecies in the Bible* (Hagerstown, MD: Review and Herald Pub. Association, 2002), 9, 10.
2   A. M. Rodriguez, *Future Glory: The 8 Greatest End-time Prophecies in the Bible*, 11.
3   A. M. Rodriguez, *Future Glory: The 8 Greatest End-time Prophecies in the Bible*, 18.
4   Ranko Stefanović, *Plain Revelation* (Berrien Springs, MI: Andrews University Press, 2013), 14.
5   Ranko Stefanović, *Plain Revelation*, 24.
6   F. B. Holbrook, *Symposium on Revelation—Book I* (Silver Spring, MD: Biblical Research Institute, General Conference of Seventh-day Adventists, 1992), 199.
7   F. B. Holbrook, *Symposium on Revelation—Book I*, 218.
8   Ranko Stefanović, *Plain Revelation*, 13.
9   F. B. Holbrook, *Symposium on Revelation—Book I*, 230.
10   F. B. Holbrook, *Symposium on Revelation—Book I*, 229.
11   F. B. Holbrook, *Symposium on Revelation—Book I*, 230.
12   B. L. Shelley, *Church History in Plain Language* (Nashville, TN: Thomas Nelson, 2013), 99.
13   Ranko Stefanović, *Plain Revelation*, 80.

14 F. B. Holbrook, *Symposium on Revelation—Book I*, 232.

15 LeRoy Froom, *The Prophetic Faith of Our Fathers, Volume I* (Hagerstown, MD: Review and Herald, 1978), 382.

16 LeRoy Froom, *The Prophetic Faith of Our Fathers, Volume I*, 382.

17 LeRoy Froom, *The Prophetic Faith of Our Fathers, Volume I*, 382.

18 LeRoy Froom, *The Prophetic Faith of Our Fathers, Volume I*, 496.

19 W. E. H. Lecky, *History of the Rise and Influence of the Spirit of Rationalism in Europe: Vol. I* (Longmans, Green, and Co., 1910), 32.

20 F. B. Holbrook, *Symposium on Revelation—Book I*, 237.

21 D. Bressan (November 1, 2011). "November 1, 1755: The Earthquake of Lisbon: Wrath of God or Natural Disaster?" (Scientific American Blog Network. Accessed November 21, 2021, https://blogs.scientificamerican. com/history-of-geology/november-1-1755-the-earthquake-of-lisbon-wr aith-of-god-or-natural-disaster/.

22 22. D. Bressan (November 1, 2011). "November 1, 1755: The Earthquake of Lisbon: Wrath of God or Natural Disaster?" "The Fowls Retired to Roost—Newburyport's Day of Darkness. Untapped History" (August 21, 2017). Accessed November 21, 2021, https://www. untappedhistory.com/single-post/2017/08/21/the-fowls-retired-to-roos t-newburyports-day-of-darkness.

23 The Stamford Historical Society Presents. "The Stamford Historical Society, Davenport Exhibit, Abraham Davenport," 1715–1789 (n.d.). Accessed November 21, 2021, https://www.stamfordhistory.org/dav_ abraham1.htm.

24 Donal O'Keeffe, "'They Thought It Was Judgment Day': The Night the Stars Fell on the Us South," *The Irish Times*, November 11, 2019, https://www.irishtimes.com/culture/they-thought-it-was-judgment-day-t he-night-the-stars-fell-on-the-us-south:1.4075652.

Chapter 6

1 Ranko Stefanović, *Plain Revelation* (Berrien Springs, MI: Andrews University Press, 2013), 163.

2 Ranko Stefanović, *Plain Revelation*, 163.

3 Sunlight Cross (n.d.), "Size of New Jerusalem." Accessed November 21, 2021, https://tourofheaven.com/eternal/new-jerusalem/size.aspx.

Printed in the United States
by Baker & Taylor Publisher Services